EXISTENTIAL
FOR AND A

EXISTENTIALISM
FOR AND AGAINST

BY

PAUL ROUBICZEK

CAMBRIDGE
AT THE UNIVERSITY PRESS
1966

PUBLISHED BY

THE SYNDICS OF THE CAMBRIDGE UNIVERSITY PRESS

Bentley House, 200 Euston Road, London, N.W. 1
American Branch: 32 East 57th Street, New York, N.Y. 10022
West African Office: P.M.B. 5181, Ibadan, Nigeria

©

CAMBRIDGE UNIVERSITY PRESS

1964

First published 1964
Reprinted 1966

Printed in Great Britain at the University Printing House, Cambridge
(Brooke Crutchley, University Printer)

PREFACE

This book is based on a selection of lectures from two courses, called *Some Aspects of Modern Philosophy* and *Towards and Beyond Existentialism*, which were given as University Extension Lectures in Cambridge under the auspices of the Board of Extra-Mural Studies of the University of Cambridge. The lectures have, however, been completely re-written to take into account the difference of style required by the spoken and the written word. But as these lectures seem to have been found helpful by a wider audience than one normally expects for philosophical lectures—an audience which included both town and gown, undergraduates and graduates, scientists and non-scientists—I have tried to recapture, even in their new version, some of the directness of the spoken word.

I wish to thank the Board of Extra-Mural Studies for arranging these courses, especially Mr. John Andrew, on whose initiative this was done, and Mr. R. J. L. Kingsford, formerly Secretary of the University Press, for encouraging me to publish them in book form.

Acknowledgments are due to two of my previous publishers for their kind permission for the use of short passages from others of my books—to Darwen Finlayson, London, for those taken from *Thinking towards Religion*, and to Charles Scribner's Sons, New York, for those from *The Misinterpretation of Man*.

Finally, I desire to express my warm gratitude and thanks to my friends Renée Payne and Douglas Hewitt who read the manuscript with meticulous care and made valuable suggestions about the form of presentation.

CLARE COLLEGE   P. R.
CAMBRIDGE
April, 1964

CONTENTS

Superior figures in the text refer to the section of references beginning on p. 185. Other notes are printed at the foot of the page.

CHAPTER I

TOWARDS EXISTENTIALISM

The need for that kind of philosophy which, to a certain extent, comes into being in Existentialism can be best understood as a reaction against the Age of Reason. For the philosophers of that age, who prided themselves upon being reasonable and rational, overstated their case in one particular respect. Reason was seen not only as man's highest faculty, capable of solving all problems and of providing him, in the end, with a complete and all-embracing knowledge, but also as entirely positive and flawless and thus as the highest product of creation. In other words, reason was considered to be absolute.

The word 'absolute' in this context means two things. First, that reason is an ultimate part of reality, underived and not determined by anything else; and second, that the powers of reason are unlimited. Thereby, however, the very belief in reason becomes irrational, for all experience shows that reason is part of human nature, that it is influenced by human nature, that its powers are limited, and that reason, therefore, cannot and must not be considered as absolute. It is this violent, unreasonable, fundamentally irrational claim of reason which in its turn produces the violent and now openly irrational reaction of Existentialism.

Belief in an absolute reason is irrational because, as I have said, all experience shows that the powers of reason have strict limitations; that a purely logical, rational, scientific way of thinking illuminates only a strictly limited sector of reality. To illustrate my meaning I should like to consider some aspects of natural science, the actual and most impressive fruit of the Age of Reason which was, after all, also the Age of Newton. The successes of science have certainly surpassed even the most optimistic expectations of that highly optimistic age. But has science proved the powers of reason to be without limits and capable of solving all problems?

Physics has probably advanced farthest of all natural sciences. Modern physicists have discovered some kind of reality behind or beyond the reality with which we are confronted, a reality of a different kind which some of them call absolute. From this 'absolute reality' they can extract certain data, for instance the basic quantum of action on which the quantum theory is based —that is, they have discovered that, for instance, energy cannot be emitted by an atom in any quantity one might like; there is a minimum quantum of it, and any quantity of energy which is actually emitted must be a multiple of this minimum quantum. This fact, however, obviously transcends reason. Why should there be these limits? The physicist must admit that there is a reality which, though it can be ascertained, can no longer be understood, or, as Heisenberg has put it, that all such knowledge is 'suspended over an unfathomable depth.'[1]

Nor will biology help in this respect. The theory of evolution, the discovery of genes, have led to great understanding of the organic world. But Darwin had to reject Lamarck's theory of evolution, and this meant that the rational had once more to give way to the irrational. Lamarck claimed that organisms adapt themselves gradually to new surroundings and new living conditions; that such acquired characteristics which enable living beings to live better are inherited and produce new species. Such a process would be understandable, but Darwin was forced to deny it, because he could find no evidence that acquired characteristics are really inherited. Instead the theory of evolution is now based on what is called mutations, sudden accidental changes in organisms which occur in an inexplicable way. Some of the new characteristics thus produced happen to be useful in the constant life and death struggle for survival; therefore individuals possessing them are selected to survive, and as they survive the new characteristics are inherited, so that new species arise. This assumption, however, is entirely irrational, for no reasonable or rational approach could enable us to understand how blind forces and accidents which alone produce the mutations that make natural selection possible could ever produce the wonderful wealth of organisms—of plants, animals and men—which exists; the mere claim that chaos and disorder could in such a way be transformed into order puts the whole process outside the boundaries of reason. Can we imagine that, if we shuffled the letters of the alphabet long enough, even for millions of years, we could ever produce *Hamlet?* Even if we could— there are calculations which seem to prove it—this is certainly not how such a play was ever written. Yet the mere shuffling of genes is credited with creating man. Evidently order can only be created by some force aiming at order, by some principle which leads to the organization of an orderly process. But most biologists warn us explicitly that we must not use the term 'purpose' when describing evolution.*

The great discovery in modern psychology, the subconscious or the unconscious, has made us recognize that human actions are determined, not only by intentions and impulses of which we are aware, but often—and more powerfully—by urges, instincts, impressions, by biological factors and childhood experiences of which we remain unaware. These are embedded in our subconscious and cannot be fully known unless they are brought to the surface by difficult procedures, and even then

* 'Purpose is a psychological term; and to ascribe purpose to a process merely because its results are somewhat similar to those of a true purposeful process is completely unjustified, and a mere projection of our own ideas into the economy of nature.' Julian Huxley, *Essays of a Biologist*, London 1923, p. 173.

our knowledge of the subconscious is slight. Obviously, however, consciousness is the basis of reason; without it reason is impossible. Therefore, if we concede the reality of the unconscious, we simultaneously concede that reason has limitations. This psychological limitation of reason is perhaps the most definitive, because the Age of Reason and its influence had been based on the identification of man with his consciousness; if the unconscious has real power—which now seems beyond doubt—reason cannot be absolute.

Even more important than such details, probably, is the fact that science, being impersonal, cannot help us when we want to deal with personal experience. Here we approach the problems with which Existentialism is concerned and can see the reasons why such a philosophy came to be developed.

In natural science quality has been reduced to quantity; thereby it has been possible to reduce dependence on the human observer who is never quite reliable, and to replace him by the more reliable method of weighing and measuring, by experiments, instruments and photographic plates. In other words, the scientific method has been made as objective as is humanly possible. The scientist himself may be passionately interested in what he is doing, but his theories are only accepted if they stand the test of impersonal observation and experiment; his feelings must needs be excluded. At the same time, this method is based on determinism, on establishing a necessary relationship between cause and effect, a relationship on which we also rely when dealing with practical affairs; we can deal with them efficiently because we are able to assume that certain causes must produce certain effects. It is true that, in modern physics, causality has been replaced by probability, but this makes little difference for practical purposes. An atomic reactor whose construction is based on the calculus of probability should work with the same exactitude as an engine constructed on the basis of classical physics. Even though some physicists (and perhaps also some biologists) no longer admit it, scientific method remains fundamentally deterministic; the sphere where causality no longer seems to operate is still made accessible with its help.*

But we cannot possibly do justice to our experiences on this basis alone; in our personal lives it is impossible to accept determinism as the only description of how cause and effect are connected. Can we really deny any freedom of the will— our freedom of choice, decision, action? Do we not feel responsible? To feel responsibility is one of our basic experiences, and Existentialism will teach us that we have to admit experience as evidence; for unless we admit that we are able to choose freely between good and evil, right and wrong, we are not responsible for our actions, and thus unable to understand what we feel. To think in a purely objective way cannot help us to deal with feelings; feelings described in an impersonal way cannot be understood. If, for instance, we are given an exact scientific description of pain, physiological and psychological, including all the processes which take place in our body and all the nerve reactions, we shall still not know what pain actually is unless we experience it. Nor will external thinking (a way of thinking, that is, which approaches everything from outside in the objective way) enable us to make reliable value-judgments, or even to grasp values at all; it can deal neither with that ultimate truth which is the basis of our convictions, for even the acceptance of scientific knowledge as the only knowledge requires a personal decision, nor with goodness or beauty. Morality is left outside because, as I have just said, without freedom of

---

* 'We could not infer the properties of the observed object from the results of measurements if the law of causality did not guarantee an unambiguous connection between the two.' W. Heisenberg, *Philosophic Problems of Nuclear Science*, p. 20.

choice and decision we are not responsible for our actions, and the whole conception of goodness and morality breaks down. If I am not responsible, murder is simply a fact, to be prevented when harmful to society and to be used when beneficial to it, but not to be judged as crime or sin. This is not a theoretical statement; all totalitarian states act upon this principle; it has become, in our age, the basis of real, of terrifying actions.

As long as external thinking alone is employed, transcendental reality, too, remains inaccessible, for the question 'Why?' can never be answered in any fundamental context. Why is there murder, why are there revolutions, or constant sources of wrath, why does man exist? We do not know, nor do we know why there is matter, the stars, the earth, nor—and this is perhaps more important—why we are born and must die, can die at any minute, and must certainly die sooner or later. Or, as Albert Camus has put it: why are we here, all of us, condemned to death? Yet obviously all these questions, when they haunt us as personal experiences, point towards some wider spiritual reality. We may never be able to answer them, but we want, at least, to find an answer to the desire for meaning. We may believe that everything is meaningless—nevertheless the quest for meaning remains an essential part of our apparently meaningless life. For there is meaning in many of our experiences, of nature and of human nature, in works of art, in books of literature or wisdom or religion; thus the urge to find meaning is so strong that it is part of our make-up, an undeniable experience. Once more we have to conclude that reason is not absolute, but limited, that belief in an absolute reason is unreasonable—and that we should find a way of thinking which could help us to deal with these hauntingly real experiences.

Of course, we could also ask: cannot these experiences—

values, freedom, the divine—be dealt with in a reasonable or even rational way? They can; but then reason is neither absolute nor all-embracing. All these experiences demand the acceptance of something which goes beyond reason—the acceptance of the limits set by our human nature, of the absolute values which can be neither derived in a rational nor proved in a scientific way, of a transcendental reality which, by definition, must transcend reason immeasurably. In short, reason must not dominate, but serve.

This is a distinction which provides another justification for Existentialism. There is the view which we have considered so far—that reason is absolute and thus dominates everything else and is the source of all our knowledge. But there is also the opposite view, and it would be difficult to reject it: that reason can also serve to elucidate something else which has to be accepted first and to which reason has then to be applied. Perhaps this difference is best explained by considering the difference between theology and philosophy, because the Age of Reason was, in the main, a rebellion against the characteristic mediaeval predominance of theology. Theology implies that we start from a given truth; theological thinking serves to interpret, explain and make understandable a truth which is accepted first. Philosophy should start from as few presuppositions as possible and help us to find out what truth is, so that truth is not the starting point, but the aim. As the Age of Reason was a reaction against theology, its philosophers tried to eliminate all presuppositions whatever, and therefore external, practical, scientific thinking seemed to be the right way to use reason. It was only thus that reason could be seen as completely autonomous; in science an unlimited advance seems to depend solely on the intellect, on logical and mathematical thinking, and its self-sufficiency seems to be confirmed by its enormous technical achievements. But this raises the obvious question: is it really possible to start without any presuppositions whatever?

There are presuppositions for the scientist, too. It is still the thinker who thinks, the knower who knows, and he is able to think and know because, in science, he starts from material reality; he does not deny that such a reality exists, but accepts and investigates it. Yet in science all these presuppositions can easily be forgotten, because its purely objective results embrace the whole external world and work miracles of technology. Nevertheless, it is dangerous to forget what is actually accepted—a danger which recurs, in a different form, in Existentialism—for the realm of man is thus more and more submerged. We need, not a reaction against theology, but a philosophy which starts from its own correct presuppositions. As we find ourselves as human beings within a material world, we can understand this world and ourselves only if we start from these given facts.

But the Age of Reason, as I have said, overlooks anything which could limit the scope of reason; man aims at knowledge, and so pays as little attention as possible to the knower. It is in vain that Pascal, the solitary rebel against that age, exclaims: 'The last proceeding of reason is to recognize that there is an infinity of things which are beyond it. It is but feeble if it does not see so far as to know this. But if natural things are beyond it, what will be said of supernatural?'[1] Descartes' dictum 'Cogito ergo sum', 'I think therefore I am', is preferred as a proof of our existence; but this proof only shows the preponderance of abstract thinking. Nowadays we see that Pascal was right; we should undoubtedly prefer to say —with Hamann, another of the predecessors of Existentialism —'Est, ergo cogito', or reversing Descartes' dictum, 'I am, therefore I think'; such a statement, however, implies an acceptance of human nature with its limitations. If I start

8

from my being, I see reason as part of it; if I accept human nature, I cannot hope that reason can solve all problems; and this is exactly what that age does not want to admit. Pascal makes us aware, on the one hand, how precarious the situation of any inner knowledge has become when, to defend his faith despite these limitations of reason, he proposes a wager. He wants you to bet that there is no God and he bets that there is one; he claims that you have nothing to lose: either you win, or, losing, you discover God—a wonderful experience which will enrich your life. A rather doubtful way of defending faith! But, on the other hand, this wager also means something else, and with that we are suddenly in the middle of Existentialism; Pascal is the first philosopher who really can be called a predecessor of the Existentialists. He uses the form of a wager in order to show that we should be committed, that we cannot approach this question in a purely objective way, because it is interconnected with inner experience. We can discuss faith meaningfully only if we are involved, if there is inner participation, if our feeling is at work.

At the beginning of the nineteenth century Kierkegaard has to go even further, since trust in an absolute reason has remained the main element in European thought. To defend his faith and his belief in an 'ethical self', in the reality of the moral law, he cannot but propose the 'absolute paradox'. This means that reason has to be dropped completely, if we want to experience and understand the sphere of values, of morality and religion. The absolute paradox means for instance that, for him, Christianity is an absurd religion because nobody, trusting reason alone, could understand that God became man and was executed as the poorest of men; but exactly because it is absurd he believes that Christianity is the best religion, for we must exercise all our powers of conviction and feeling to be able to embrace this faith. We must take what he calls a leap into the unknown, a jump into the abyss. As we cannot rely on reason, we can force no one into belief, not even ourselves; but the one thing we can and must do is to take the risk—to give up all the results of rational thinking, of scientific reasoning, and to surrender to the inner voice which tells us that there is a different reality, a sphere of a different kind, transcending reason. If we do that, so Kierkegaard believes, we shall jump into the open arms of God. And it is he who coins the word 'Existentialism'.

All this shows, of course, that the overemphasis on the rational is being replaced by an overemphasis on the irrational; that the reaction is going too far. Yet it can hardly be denied that the reaction had become necessary, and that there are positive elements in it.

What does the word 'Existentialism' mean? This new kind of philosophy is pursued by many philosophers from whom a number of different schools derive their origin, which makes the meaning of the word rather confusing. But its original and fundamental meaning, in the sense of Kierkegaard's usage of it, is simple and straightforward. Existentialism is a rejection of all purely abstract thinking, of a purely logical or scientific philosophy; in short, a rejection of the absoluteness of reason. Instead it insists that philosophy should be connected with the individual's own life and experience, with the historical situation in which he finds himself, and that it should be, not interesting abstract speculation, but a way of life. It should be a philosophy capable of being lived. All this is summed up in the word 'existence'. The Existentialist philosopher insists that what I really know is not the external world as such, but my own experience; for him the personal is the real. Philosophy, therefore, should start from one's own experience, one's own inner knowledge, and it is inner knowledge which should be qualified, enlarged, and in this way enriched. One's own experience must be admitted as evidence. Reason, as some of the less extreme Existentialists show, can serve this approach, but it must never dictate.

Perhaps it is easier to understand what Existentialism means when, as is often done, we introduce the distinction between essence and existence. Essence refers to the true nature of things, the humanness of man, the horseness of a horse. It can be considered in an abstract way. Existence is not the humanity of man, but this man John whom I know, or this particular horse which I possess and love. Now the Existentialists claim that all preceding philosophy was too much concerned with essences, with ideas, with concepts, and that it thus became too abstract. They want to start from existence and to keep to it, so that the real things are kept intact, as intact as they occur in our actual personal experience. There is no doubt that Existentialists often go too far in their exclusive emphasis on existence; to achieve true understanding we obviously need both, essence and existence. We shall not understand man without understanding his humanity, but neither shall we understand humanity without paying attention to single men and to our own inner experience. The claim that one can deal with existence alone is as much a fallacy as the claim that dealing with essences alone does justice to reality. But even if the reaction of some of these thinkers was too strong, we can still see that it was necessary and wholesome.

In a rather contradictory way, the Age of Reason is still with us. We certainly no longer believe that reason can solve all problems; perhaps we even find its deification ridiculous. The discovery of the subconscious was a shock from which belief in reason never completely recovered. Yet our age is still largely dominated by abstract thinking, by impersonal, scientific, deterministic thought, by concentration on essences, by rationalism. We rarely pay enough attention to the deeper meaning of our personal experience and of our feelings; we disregard inner knowledge, but we are beginning to feel, I believe, that this emphasis on abstract thought is impoverishing or even endangering the human world. The whole world seems to lose significance, and man is estranged from himself. Our domination over nature is becoming more and more complete; man can make use of the most minute particles and, perhaps soon, of outer space; he is encroaching on the very structure of the universe and, by means of new medical techniques and new drugs, on human character. Yet while the enigmas of nature are solved one by one, each man becomes to himself a greater enigma, and there is more and more chaos in our own inner lives and in human affairs. Are we still able to solve moral problems? It would probably be more important than ever before to develop morality, since we are confronted with an entirely new situation. Nuclear warfare may interfere with human existence, with the mystery of life and death, to an extent never thought possible before. The power to interfere with man's character brings with it a new and very great responsibility. All such problems, however, are outside the scope of science; we cannot begin to grasp their true meaning as long as we rely on abstract thought alone.

Obviously, man loses his foothold in reality once he loses his belief in values, once he cannot trust anything higher than man, once there is no transcendental basis for his spiritual experiences. As an impersonal approach, moreover, cannot make accessible feelings which are nothing if not personal, an essential part of all our experiences is made to appear negligible. Everything we fully experience, however, is accompanied by feelings; we cannot be alive without them; and if they are disregarded, they are damaged.

No science can be of help here, not even psychology. It is true that it includes all such problems, but only a particular aspect of them—and this does not help us to find a foothold, because everything is made relative. Value-judgments are seen as the results of social pressures and personal predelictions, faith is an outcome of inferiority complexes. This may be true in many special cases; but is it the whole truth? Nietzsche, who was certainly a great psychologist, once called our virtues the hiding places of our vices and showed how often our virtues are simply used to hide ulterior motives. Again, this is often true; but whence does Nietzsche get the concepts 'virtue' and 'vice'? They are, in this context, presupposed. Psychology includes only processes of thought and feelings, we are told *how* we think and feel, but the actual content of thought goes beyond its reach; the concepts 'virtue' and 'vice' are to be found on a deeper level which is not touched by psychology. Virtue may be misused, belief in God founded upon a wrong reaction, yet there may be true virtue and God may exist. To decide questions of truth and falsehood we need another criterion. I may help a friend for purely selfish reasons, because I enjoy it or because it is useful for me; yet to help another person still may—or may not—be a good principle.

Psychoanalysis increases the one-sidedness of psychology in a striking way. Its original impulse was to remove all the hindrances due to subconscious factors which make a patient unable to face life properly, so as to restore his freedom of decision and action. It is still used thus by good doctors. But if you look at theoretical psychoanalytic writings you will find that, despite these original intentions, they tend to support determinism. They mainly show how dependent we are on such factors as childhood experiences upon which we had no influence, and how these factors, at work in the subconscious, prevent free actions. In fact, psychoanalysis has developed as a challenge to its own basic tenet and has provided some of the strongest arguments against any belief in the freedom of will. This is a natural outcome of the scientific method; it is bound to work in the direction of establishing causality; the more fully we disclose a necessary connexion between cause and effect, the better use we have made of this method, and the better will it enable us to solve practical problems. As the method is designed to disclose necessity, freedom can never be proved in this way; to discover it we must start from experience.

Therefore, we must genuinely start from experience. Nothing, not even a strong belief in such theories, will ever convince a man, in the small affairs of everyday life, that he is unable to do what he wants to do; if he feels inhibited in small, practical actions he will see a doctor or psychiatrist because he will know that there is something wrong with him. And what is true of small actions, must be true of more important actions, of moral decisions, too. Despite all the powerful external and internal compulsions which often defeat us we shall not understand man unless we take into account his freedom as well. The theories supporting determinism actually provide one of the most surprising proofs for the reality of the feeling of responsibility which presupposes freedom. This feeling, to say the least, is more often than not disagreeable, and there are now many respectable theories which we could use as an excuse for shunning responsibility, theories which show that we are moulded by innumerable influences, so that we are bound to be what we are and cannot help it. Yet, in actual practice, the theories prove to be no excuse; in spite of them, responsibility remains; we still feel responsible and insist that man ought to feel responsible. Thus, to understand man, we really cannot avoid the attempt to do justice to this feeling.

There is no escape from embarking upon a personal philosophy; not even our 'historical sense', another of our achievements, will help us to evade some kind of existential approach. Knowledge of history, too, has greatly developed since the Age of Reason. That age did not think historically; everything was judged by contemporary standards; history showed only the stages which led to its crowning product, namely to that age itself. Now we see everything in historical perspective, evaluating achievements within the framework of their historical conditions, and thus appreciating them more fully. There is no doubt that this is a great advance; but can it help us to find firm ground to stand upon? When we rely on history alone, everything once again becomes relative. We can only discover, in each age, certain basic beliefs which appeared to men as so self-evident that there was no need to think further, and which then, in the next age, had to be dismissed as insufficient. We never discover basic truth. All values and all beliefs, right and wrong, religion, Christianity, simply become historical phenomena; history as such cannot tell us anything about their validity. Morality appears as the mere product of social, national, historical conditions, changing like fashions; 'right and justice, fraternity and liberty' as a 'lip-service to modern mythological gods', as Marx said. We are reduced to helpless pawns in a huge gamble, arranged by unknown, meaningless powers, to which we must submit. We cannot believe in anything, and, to quote Albert Camus again, 'If we believe in nothing, if nothing has meaning and if we can affirm no values whatsoever, then everything is possible and nothing has any importance. The murderer is neither right nor wrong. Evil and virtue are mere chance or caprice.'[1] This, however, is the impasse brought about when only scientific or historical thinking is accepted and all personal experience disregarded. Then we have to do what the opportunity demands, and we are bound to ask with Camus: 'Who will decide on the opportunity, if not the opportunist?'[2]

In short, unless there are absolute standards which are valid for every man, something which stands higher than man and can lift him above the flux of events, above the influences upon which he himself has no influence, man remains submerged in the world and cannot assert himself. He cannot live a life which could be called personal.

The fact, however, that values, standards, morality, faith are needed is no proof that they are real, that we are entitled to accept them. Is there any basis for such an acceptance, or are they mere wishful thinking? This is a question which we shall raise again and again. We shall try, as objectively as we can, to test the actual elements in our experience, their nature, their trustworthiness, the justification of our beliefs, the significance of the personal and impersonal approach, and to do so objectively, we shall also constantly pay attention to scientific achievements and try to see how far these can help us.

We shall not rely on the Existentialists alone; as they often go too far, they often let us down. Reacting against the absolute claims of reason, they make absolute claims for the irrational; instead of scientific or rational thought they passionately embrace everything irrational and expect thus to find absolute knowledge. This absoluteness, too, leads into the void, and it is this void, nothingness, *le Néant, das Nichts,* which is then proclaimed paradoxically as the highest good. The intention of this book is to find the basis for an equilibrium, a way out of this violent interplay of action and reaction which has always driven European thought into one-sidedness; the reaction of the Age of Reason against the Middle Ages just as much as the reaction of Existentialism against rationalism. We shall keep in mind that, in the end, we want to establish a balance; and because this is our intention, we shall concentrate rather on the positive aspects of Existentialism than on its dangers and exaggerations, though these will be mentioned too. To some extent, some such reaction was undoubtedly necessary, and this is the aspect of Existentialism which interests us most. We want to find positive results which we are entitled to accept—a task which points both towards and beyond Existentialism.

CHAPTER II

PROGRESS OR CATASTROPHE

DARWIN AND NIETZSCHE

The main creed of the nineteenth century was belief in progress in its modern form—not simply belief that there will be progress if we make proper use of our gifts and strive for the right aims, but a conviction that progress is automatic and inevitable. According to that belief, humanity has developed and is bound to continue to develop in the right direction, towards better and better forms of social and personal life, and in nature, too, a steady development from lower to higher forms is constantly bound to occur. Progress is first seen as an historical, later as a natural law. There may be occasional digressions or retrogressions, but they will never be important enough to halt progress or even to delay it seriously.

Perhaps it is useful to remember that the idea of progress is of fairly recent origin and neither as old nor as self-evident as it may appear to us. Whole civilizations have been without it. The older civilizations looked backwards to a golden age, to a paradise lost—that is, to a perfect beginning; they did not look forward to the future. Christianity was responsible for such a concentration on the future; the second coming of Christ, however, was not promised as logical outcome of increasing human perfection; the original prophecy insisted that He would return amidst the greatest catastrophes mankind has ever witnessed—a prophecy which, promising that the worst can bring about the best, may once again become a greater consolation than trust in an unlimited progression of human achievements. An explicit belief in progress began to develop in the Age of Reason, though in that age it was seen as the consequence of the correct application of reason and not as a matter of course. It is only in the nineteenth century that this hope was transformed, though not without some difficulty, into a law.

During that century Europe became more and more intoxicated by the sudden and rapid advance of the natural sciences; it is hardly surprising, therefore, that progress should have appeared as a general law. It is worth remembering how many important discoveries which seem rather long established to us were made as recently as the nineteenth century. To mention just a few examples of such discoveries: the law of the conservation of energy; spectrum analysis, which shows that all stars consist of the same materials; electric waves, which were to transform life on this earth; the periodic law, which makes of chemistry a science; the origin of human beings from egg cells. Add to these the industrial revolution, the world of railways and later of the telegraph, the development of medicine, and one can understand why the Europeans of that time could believe so firmly that progress was inevitable.

The law of progress was first propounded by Hegel who founded it upon an idealistic basis. Hegel's influence on the further development of European thought is profound, but though he even prepared the way for scientific thinking, his idealism did not appeal directly to the natural scientists. For them, there was still an important gap which made belief in progress difficult—the wealth of organisms, the existence of innumerable plants and animals and the emergence of man remained inexplicable. There it still seemed necessary to turn to the Bible, to the story of creation, for any explanation at all. This gap, however, was filled in 1859 by the appearance of Darwin's *The Origin of Species*, and thus it is understandable why this book had such a striking success practically over night. At long last it was possible to explain everything in the normal, scientific, mechanical way, the Bible finally became superfluous in the realm of science, and, now that it could also be seen at work in nature, the existence of progress seemed to have been proved conclusively.

It is not my task to discuss the theory of evolution as such, its validity, its details and its transformation since Darwin, but only its philosophical implications. It exercised a very great influence upon philosophy. Materialism was changed; all materialistic teachings since then, including that of Marx, are based on the theory of evolution. Philosophers like Herbert Spencer made this theory the basis of all philosophy, of metaphysics, psychology, ethics; Nietzsche was more influenced by it than he admitted; Henri Bergson, though fundamentally an idealist, succumbed to it; even theologians who struggled against its misapplication took it for granted. This influence of Darwin upon philosophy has diminished only since the advent of Existentialism, and it has not diminished very much.

The significance of the theory for philosophy consists mainly in its seeming to provide a consistent and all-inclusive metaphysical system, explaining better than previous systems both the universe and the existence of man. It is true that the origin of matter is not explained, but some such presupposition has to be accepted in all systems; Plato, after all, started from the existence of spiritual entities, from ideas, Hegel from the conception of an all-embracing spirit, and the materialists start from the existence of matter. But this first basic assumption can easily be overlooked because man is fascinated by the power of the human mind to build such a system, and the fascination is perhaps greatest in the case of the theory of evolution, for this system seems to be supported by the discovery of more and more facts. No wonder that it was considered to be ultimate, absolute knowledge.

Once the existence of matter is accepted, the theory of evolution seems to make it possible to explain everything else without further assumptions, without any outside interference from a creator or divine being. There seems to be no need for the transcendental. Accidents and blind forces produce deviations in organic forms; at the same time there are more living beings than food; therefore a life and death struggle for survival develops and those individuals which by accident are better equipped for this struggle survive. By this natural selection new species evolve. Thus purely mechanical forces gradually produce, over millions of years, all the organisms we know, and in the end man. In the course of the development they also produce the mind which contributes to fitness and which therefore also grows; thus even the existence of reason is explained. The emphasis is entirely on accidents and blind forces. We have mentioned before that biologists do not want us to use the term 'purpose'; Julian Huxley, for instance, is very explicit in his insistence on the mechanical aspect of evolution: 'There are the vast powers of inorganic nature, neutral or hostile to man. Yet they gave birth to evolving life, whose development, though blind and fortuitous, has tended in the same general direction as our own conscious desires and ideals, and so gives us an external sanction for our directional activities. This again gave birth to human mind.'[1]

Of course, there are gaps. It is not only the existence of matter which has to be presupposed, but also the occurrence of some inexplicable irregularity. According to one theory, matter was originally extremely concentrated, according to another thinly spread throughout the whole of space; in both cases some irregularity had to produce movement, so as to bring into being the universe we know. Thus, as we have said, disorder must produce order, which cannot be rationally justified.* There are two more gaps which Julian Huxley never omits to mention: the origin of life, and despite all attempts to minimize it, that of the different quality of the human mind. But one need only read Huxley to see how easily even these major gaps can be disregarded. There are, in fact, more gaps still; it is not known, for instance, how new species actually arise. Darwin assumed that there are gradual, imperceptible changes which produce new species, but this theory has since been dismissed; instead the origin of species is now based on sudden changes, mutations, which, if useful, are inherited and produce new species; but it is still not known why these irregularities occur. The main problem of the theory, the origin of species, still defies satisfactory explanation, and we can still say with Darwin that our ignorance of the laws of change is profound.

These gaps are not crucial as long as we are concerned with the scientific theory. It is important to remember that biologists speak of a *theory* of evolution, and that we ought always to bear in mind that it is a theory; single facts have been discovered, but the link between them is an assumption, a hypothesis. As a scientific hypothesis, the idea of evolution is extremely useful; it helps to explain facts to such an extent that further fruitful research becomes possible. But, as with all theories, the scientist has to be prepared to change it if new discoveries are made which do not agree with it, or to replace it altogether if it cannot be adapted to the discoveries. After all, there have been important changes since Darwin, such as the introduction of the concept of mutations and of genes; sooner or later such modifications of the theory may affect the fundamental idea itself. In other words: the theory of evolution

* See p. 3.

shows, as do all theories, the limitations of knowledge; it should not, therefore, be accepted as a complete basis for philosophy or as ultimate, absolute truth. Scientists are fully entitled to make it the basis of research, but philosophers should consider its limitations critically.

Nevertheless, evolution has been made the basis of a complete philosophy; it provided philosophers with a metaphysical and ethical system, thus deeply influencing their ideas about the nature of man and his behaviour. In fact, the philosophy based on Darwinism has exercised an extremely strong influence, far beyond the realms of science and philosophy, upon the whole development of European thought. The ruthless life and death struggle for survival has been translated into a new morality, as ruthless competition in the capitalist, as ruthless class warfare in the communist world, and as ruthless nationalism everywhere. Moreover, for the first time in human history, mind and reason are no longer seen as some mysterious higher power, as part of a supernatural, divine sphere breaking in upon human existence, but as the product of lower, biological factors, and nothing has done more to fortify materialism. The word 'spirit' has all but lost its meaning, and the human mind itself has been impoverished. For, though we may discuss endlessly what is the real difference between animals and man, there is no doubt that man is the only animal which is influenced by its idea of itself, so that the lowering of the status of reason has lowered the status of man and undermined the foundations of his dignity. Reason, initially considered as absolute and capable of solving all problems, finally seems to remove all problems by degrading itself.

To appreciate what this philosophy means in terms of human life and experience, we had best turn to the philosophy of Nietzsche. It may sound suprising that I should wish to link Nietzsche so directly with Darwin, but I hope to show that to understand Nietzsche's indebtedness to Darwin is to understand more fully the nineteenth century's belief in progress.

It is true that Nietzsche, a great admirer of the French, despises the English, and this contempt comes to the fore in his ferocious attack on Darwin. Darwin appears to him as a meek Englishman of mediocre intelligence, whose 'incomprehensibly one-sided doctrine' is submerged 'in something very like the stuffy air of English overpopulation, something very like the smell of the want and the cramped life of the poor.'[1] Nevertheless, Darwin's influence on Nietzsche's philosophy, despite certain deviations from it and certain criticisms, is very strong indeed, especially on that part of it which leads to the creation of the ideal of the superman. It is most helpful, therefore, to trace how Nietzsche arrives at his ideal, since he sees more clearly than most what is needed to transform the theory of evolution into a complete philosophy. There is certainly no doubt—even for those who reject his philosophy —that Nietzsche was one of the most acute and far-sighted thinkers; and as he is also in many ways a predecessor of the Existentialists, he never fails to show what abstract terms mean when translated into human experience.

If man is to be entirely understood as the product of biological evolution, everything he does has to be explained as an effect of his physiological make-up; moral standards and values must be shown to be relative, because they are dependent on these conditions. One has to admit that, as Nietzsche says, 'Moral values are delusive values compared with physiological ones.'[2] To be able to follow this line of thought, Nietzsche makes psychology the basis of his approach to all problems, for this is the best tool if one wants to show how far we are influenced by motives of which we remain unaware. He is an excellent psychologist, though he concentrates mainly on this self-delusory aspect of man's thinking and behaviour. He never fails to lay bare those regions of the human mind which are 'all too human'. Man's noblest endeavours are exposed as masks covering his animal instincts. Where before men thought they were witnessing enthusiasm and a wealth of admirable feeling, 'sick feelings' and a 'cruel voluptuousness' are uncovered, and the very virtues are recognized as the meeting place of crass egotism, indifference, dishonesty and lust for power. There is no enjoyment of things for their own sake, but only 'the enjoyment of oneself through things'.[1] We are illogical and unjust beings whose gratitude is 'a milder form of revenge,'[2] and whose pity, allied almost without exception with envy, is only the way by which the weak can win power, 'the power to hurt'.[3] Nearly all the motives which we profess publicly serve only to hide the real mainsprings of our actions; 'we shall seldom err when we ascribe extreme actions to vanity, mediocre actions to habit, and petty ones to fear'.[4] Belief means nothing, for it is only 'the adoption of guiding principles without reasons',[5] and 'men believe in the truth of everything which is visibly, strongly believed'.[6] Even the universality of a faith is in no way conclusive: 'To help a doctrine to victory often means only so to mix it with stupidity that the weight of the latter carries off the victory of the former.'[7]

By this unambiguous attitude Nietzsche reveals himself as accepting a fallacy—a fallacy to which he has to succumb in order to make the theory of evolution a philosophy, and his error is most revealing because the fallacy, in many different contexts, is still with us. We have referred before to his description of virtues and vices;* these concepts are obviously taken from outside the sphere of psychology which is

* See p. 13.

concerned with the processes of thought, not with fundamental concepts. All that Nietzsche says is often true, but it is not the whole truth; there is a deeper level of thought beyond the realm of psychological reactions. It is no accident that the enumeration of vices—egotism, indifference, dishonesty, lust of power—tallies fairly exactly with everyone's idea of vices; judgments are implied, and judgments are based on standards and convictions. One can show, with the help of psychology, how standards work, how they are used or misused, but their origin lies elsewhere. To give a modern example which may elucidate the necessary—and in this kind of philosophy necessarily omitted—differentiation still further: psychoanalysts claim that belief in God is frequently based on the father-complex, that men growing up miss the protection of their father and the awe of him which they experienced in childhood, and that therefore they invent a father in heaven to replace him. That may be true of quite a number of people, but it does not prove the existence or the non-existence of a god. People arrive at a belief in God in many ways, and some of them may be false; but the question of the existence of God must be decided on different grounds. It is obviously wrong to use one particular psychological phenomenon as a proof for the non-existence of God.

Yet it is exactly in this way that Nietzsche achieves what is required to make the biological theory the basis of philosophy, namely to discredit morality. Evidently, if we are to embark on a life and death struggle for survival, morality is of no significance; and if there is progress, automatic and inevitable progress, morality must be worthless, too. If everything which happens is bound to make things better and better, it would be sheer folly, it would even be wicked, to hinder this wonderful process for the sake of immaterial moral scruples. Therefore, morality has to be discarded, and that is what Nietzsche does, basing the dismissal on his psychological insight. If all virtues are nothing but pretence, then morality is not what we claim it to be, the outcome of an absolute moral law, the conscious embodiment of real values, but an excuse, serving the particular purpose of hiding motives which ought to be recognized for what they are—ulterior motives. For their hidden purpose is the defeat of the strong by the weak.

This is the constant scheme which underlies Nietzsche's attacks on morality and Christianity; both are seen as vicious because they make it impossible for the strong man to be, as he should, master. We shall discuss the ideal of the strong man in a moment; it is obvious from the start, however, how much this ideal fits in with the conditions of the life and death struggle for survival, whose necessary implications are merely brought into the open. If the natural order—which would then necessarily be the ideal order—were left intact, all those who are weak would be subjugated by those who are strong; to defend themselves, according to Nietzsche, the weak ones therefore invented what we usually accept as normal or Christian morality. This morality is more easily obeyed by a weak man than by a strong one who has vigorous instincts and urges, and if it is made the highest standard the weak man appears to be the superior being. Thus all our morality is seen as a slave morality, a morality of the herd, destined to break down the healthy man so that he may be subjugated. 'The European disguises himself in morality, because he has become a sick, sickly, crippled animal who has good reasons for being "tame", because he is almost an abortion, an imperfect, weak and clumsy thing.'[1] Religion is a neurosis which produces and makes use of this illness. With Christianity, especially, begins 'the slave-insurrection in morals'[2] which has justified and won over all those who are 'misfits, the badly favoured, all the scum and the outcasts of mankind'.

Improvement in the Christian sense is the very opposite of real improvement, for it means that men are 'tamed, weakened, discouraged, softened, enfeebled, emasculated'. Christianity 'crushed and broke man entirely and submerged him as in a slough of mud'.[1] Only 'beyond good and evil' does real life begin.

Much of this criticism of morality and Christianity is well worth heeding, for instance the reproach that, while the Buddhist behaves and acts in a way different from that of the non-Buddhist, the Christian behaves and acts like everyone else and possesses a religion of ceremonies and moods which he keeps separate from his everyday life. (The next chapter will be devoted to a discussion of the positive aspects of Nietzsche's philosophy.) But he goes much further, and his next step fits in once more with the demands of philosophical Darwinism; God has to be dismissed as well. He emphasizes again and again: 'God is dead', and asks rhetorically: 'What thinker still needs the hypothesis of God?'[2] He attacks all religions without reservation: 'Never yet has a religion contained a truth, neither directly nor indirectly, neither as dogma nor as symbol.'[3] Thus the way is open for the rule of accidents and blind forces—and for the uninhibited praise of the strong man.

Pity for the weak is foolish. Slavery was always 'a condition of every higher culture',[4] and 'egotism is necessary if there are to be noble souls'. The man who develops culture looks different from the picture which Christians and moralists have of him. 'He handles lies, violence, the most ruthless egotism as his tools with such mastery that he could only be called an evil and demonic being.'[5] The 'more complete men' were always the 'more complete beasts'.[6] Forbearance and peace are enfeebling; war has to be accepted as something positive, for 'war is the father of all good'[7]—a slight mistranslation from the Greek which is meant to show that war is 'indispensable'.[1] 'In renouncing war one has renounced the great life'.[2] We must breed in man a new kind of conscience so that we associate our traditional virtues with a bad conscience, and strength and power with a good conscience. Man must strive to become 'a beast of prey, the magnificent blond beast greedily roaming after booty and victory ... The animal must emerge again, and go back to the jungle ... It is the noble races which, wherever they went, have left in their tracks the concept of "Barbarian".'[3] Vitality as such, which appeared so desirable to the nineteenth century, triumphs without reservations.

Acceptance of biological standards must needs make sheer vitality a value of the highest order, but it is rarely connected with praise of the beast of prey and the barbarian. Yet the extreme statement once more throws light on essential aspects of this attitude. Before embarking on a description of the final ideal, however, a few points should be mentioned, to show the logical—or rather illogical—support which any such creed requires.

Nietzsche's earlier philosophy aims at establishing the claim that 'nothing is true', so that, therefore, 'everything is permitted'. Nothing is true because, if all depends on the needs of the species, there is no constant, absolute truth, but merely changing physiological requirements. Such a statement, however, is a contradiction, and one we can never escape when trying to make relativity all-embracing. Nietzsche defines truth as 'that kind of error without which a certain species of living beings could not exist'.[4] But this assertion, to have any meaning at all, has to be really and absolutely true. This is the fallacy of all relative truths when they are considered as fundamental; in the last resort they must still be based on something which is considered as true, for otherwise they cannot even be discussed meaningfully. Nietzsche warns us: 'Life is no argument; error might be among the conditions of life,'[1] but this very life against which he warns us is for him an infallible measure. He does believe in a number of absolute truths; in heredity, for instance, and he certainly considers his psychology to be infallible. He commits a similar fallacy when he establishes his claim that 'everything is permitted'. He wants to get away from the word 'law', which seems to him to imply conventional morality: 'There is no law; every power acts at each moment in utter accordance with its nature.' But this, if anything, is again the formulation of a law, the more so as he himself adds: 'The fact that nothing else is possible is the basis of calculability.'[2] He actually wants to perform a 'revaluation of all values', to establish a new law and a new morality, for it is impossible to act without any code of behaviour. If we deny absolute truth and accepted morality, even if only because we want to be cautious and realistic and avoid unjustified assertions, we help to bring about that belief in expediency and opportunism against which Camus has warned us*—a belief very little different from that implied in the acceptance of the 'blond beast', in spite of all the endeavours of Nietzsche to make the strong man noble.

There is another side to these endeavours, too. Nietzsche wants to escape from all conventions and prejudices, so as to be able to face life directly, without any presuppositions—an admirable and courageous attempt which, as we shall see in the next chapter, is in many ways fruitful. But even he is unable to start without any presuppositions. His praise of vitality is obviously influenced by the fear of decadence which seized Europe at the end of the nineteenth century—the fear that the health and biological strength of European man

* See p. 15.

had been undermined by his intellectual development to such an extent that his survival was endangered. This fear can be recognized everywhere: in France the cult of the 'fin de siècle' was typical, and this feeling spread to England, where fear of decadence can be seen in the work, for example, of D. H. Lawrence. Russia was warned by many writers against accepting the Western way of life because the West seemed doomed. In Germany, under Schopenhauer's and Nietzsche's influence, the young Thomas Mann, Stefan George and others expressed the same fear. The 'blond beast' is meant as an antidote. For us it is probably difficult to recapture this fear which dominated many of the best minds of the time, because decadence did not set in; European man has survived two world wars in excellent biological health, though he may have become more of a barbarian again— but this is a different matter. Yet the fear was so strong then that Nietzsche even tried to counteract it by a dogmatic statement: 'This world is the Will to Power—and nothing else. And even you yourselves are this will to power— and nothing besides'[1]—a dogma which loses much of its appeal once the fear is gone.*

The emphasis on the will to power, however, is also important in itself. The fear of decadence certainly aggravated the ruthless struggle for survival in human society. In seeing it also as the effect of the will to power Nietzsche indicates another impulse which is at work—the attempt to make man a god. Christianity had concentrated attention so entirely on God-man that now that 'God is dead' He has to be replaced by making man a god. This urge is probably most clearly expressed by one of Dostoevsky's characters who speaks like Nietzsche before Nietzsche had developed these ideas. In *The Possessed*, Kirillov is convinced that 'there is no God', and

---

* This statement has, of course, metaphysical implications, but here I am not concerned with these.

concludes: 'If God exists, all is His will and from His will I cannot escape. If not, it's all my will and I am bound to show self-will . . . If there is no god, then I am God.'[1] Or, as Nietzsche puts it: 'If there were gods how could I bear it to be no god myself? Therefore, there are no gods.'[2] Is it unreasonable to wonder whether the same motive can be felt behind the enormous impetus of modern natural science and technology, and does it not account for much in our age? Man, deprived of the divine, is bound to reach out for powers once considered divine.

This may seem self-contradictory, because scientific thinking, as we have said, must aim at determinism, and inescapable historical and natural laws are the basis of the theory of evolution. But this contradiction only goes to confirm that it is humanly impossible to accept determinism completely.* Determinism implies that free will does not exist, because all happenings, including those which seem to be the free actions of man, are determined by external necessity. However, all teachings based on determinism appeal to man to act in accordance with this teaching—that is, they appeal to his free will. Julian Huxley, dismissing purpose in favour of blind forces and accidents, yet wants us to practice eugenics;† Karl Marx, for whom communism is not an aim or ideal, but 'the actual trend of events' brought about by necessity, yet wants his followers to make revolutions. It is not surprising that Nietzsche's desire to make man a god is characteristic of attempts which, though utterly different in their form and object, rest on the same foundations.

His new god is the superman, the noble barbarian who combines the beauty and strength of the animal with great intellectual powers which will enable him to conquer himself, the masses, the world, and even fate. He is to be the master of

* See pp. 14.   † See quotations beginning p. 36.

the earth, fulfilling 'the mission of the earth', giving meaning to history. Dancing serenity and deepest seriousness are to be allied to insensitive cruelty and a great power of suffering. He, as the final embodiment of the will to power, is allowed to kill and must live near to crime. We cannot yet imagine all his splendour, but all the great geniuses allow us a glimpse of what is to come.

This thought is, up to a point, caused by the theory of evolution which, in its scientific form, contains one more unexplained gap which we have not yet mentioned. As a natural law, evolution should be a continual process; but it seems to reach its summit in man and ceases to function further. The superman is obviously Nietzsche's attempt to deal with this omission. He tries—consciously or unconsciously —to anticipate the next step, to discover how man could develop further. What is more important, however, is that the vision of the superman re-establishes an age-old ideal.

Since the superman belongs to a far away future, it is understandable that the description of him remains vague; by definition, he must transcend all actual knowledge. But there is one genius whom Nietzsche admires so much that we feel that the superman is fashioned upon the image of this man— Napoleon. Of his achievements Nietzsche says that they are 'almost the history of the higher happiness . . . which has been achieved in this century in its most valuable men and moments . . . He has brought again to the surface a whole part of the antique character, and what is perhaps the most important part,' and thus he has introduced a new era. 'We owe it to Napoleon . . . that several centuries of war, unequalled in history, may now follow each other; in short, that we have entered the classical age of war . . . upon which all the following centuries will look back with envy and awe as on a manifestation of perfection.'[1]

The superman represents above all the great warrior, the ruthless conqueror. It is true that, in the last quotation, we also begin to see the 'other' Nietzsche, the prophet who warns us of coming dangers; while most believers in progress thought that wars belonged to the past and that the twentieth century would see the millenium, he was one of the few who foresaw 'the age of war' and was—unfortunately—right. But at first he welcomes these wars because he wants the superman to be a great warrior and the world to accept his absolute power. The prevailing worship of Napoleon had already shown that admiration of warlike heroism reached a new peak as Christian faith lost its hold over Europe. It was able to return because it is precisely on this point that Christianity failed to convert the European; to be a hero remained a supreme aim even in the Middle Ages when the strange ideal of chivalry combined Christianity (which demands that one must not kill and ought to love one's enemy) with the idealization of battle. But Nietzsche is the first who gives to this attitude a conscious and seductive modern expression; with him this norm of greatness—heroic man as master of the masses and as conqueror of the world—becomes one of the most powerful agents in recent history.

It is mainly for this reason that Nietzsche has been accused of being a predecessor of the Nazis and acclaimed by them as their philosopher. This is, of course, a one-sided interpretation; there is another side to Nietzsche, too, which we shall have to emphasize in the next chapter; to a large extent, however, the accusation is justified. Those defending the superman point out that he is also represented as a serene dancer, as being in love with life, as lighthearted and laughing, yet his lightheartedness is always forced, and if we try to apply the underlying ideas to real men the probable result is rather an heroic storm trooper than the idealized Zarathustra who combined within himself incompatible qualities. Although Nietzsche only gave fuller expression to ideas which were already at work in his time, there can be no doubt that his teaching contributed essentially to their disastrous development.

The ideal of the superman becomes particularly pernicious as a result of one factor introduced because of the influence of Darwin—by Nietzsche's belief in heredity. His belief is much more dogmatic than it would be for most scientists; once more, however, the extreme statement throws into sharp relief the consequences of basing a philosophy upon the theory of evolution. Nietzsche believes that other influences are powerless against heredity. 'If you know something about the parents, then you may draw conclusions about the child... and with the best instruction and education you can only succeed in deceiving others about such an inheritance.'[1] Yet if instruction and education are hopeless, then the only way of arriving at a higher race, at the superman, is by breeding. This is the consequence which Nietzsche demands, and he says with complete clarity what it means. He praises the religious rules of the lowest Indian caste, the Chandala, 'the fruit of adultery, incest and crime', because these rules see to it that these people are gradually annihilated by 'deadly epidemics and the most ghastly venereal diseases', for this annihilation of the lower caste is 'the necessary consequence of the concept of breeding.' He continually demands the breeding of a new master-race and the prohibition, for its sake, of the reproduction of all 'the discontented, the rancorous and the grudging', the sterilization of criminals and 'the annihilation of millions of misfits.'[2] The spectre of the Nazi gas chambers looms behind such statements.

Undoubtedly, it would be an undue simplification to ascribe to the influence of a single philosopher the rise of one of the most criminal and evil systems ever witnessed. Yet, equally undoubtedly, the fact that a philosopher of great repute had expressed such demands made it easier to translate them into action. However, we must not forget that it is not only Nietzsche's philosophy, but also the theory of evolution which leads to such consequences. Nietzsche's theories about the breeding of a superman ought to act as a warning against a much more common attitude, which can be seen when, for example, we turn once more to Julian Huxley.

Huxley is well-meaning and wants to be humane. He sees the dangers of the superman: 'I certainly do not want to see man erected into the position of a god, as happened with many individual human beings in the past and is still happening to-day.' But he believes that 'it seems now to be established that people with higher intelligence have, on the average, a lower reproductive rate than the less intelligent. If this process were to continue, the results would be extremely grave. Society needs more intelligent people.' He also believes that 'artificial selection can be much more effective and can get results much more quickly than natural selection'—a theory which he proves with horses. He therefore concludes: 'The geneticist knows that with appropriate methods, such a result could be achieved over a measurable series of generations. Admittedly, this could not happen without *somewhat* radical changes in customs and laws and outlook ... Once the fact is grasped that we men are the agents of further evolution, and that there can be no action higher or more noble than raising the inherent possibilities of life, ways and means will *somehow* be found for overcoming any resistances that stand in the way of that realization ... large scale eugenics ... can become an incentive and a hope.'[1] Can the 'somewhat' and 'somehow' mean anything but Nietzsche's methods of breeding?

Huxley tries to introduce safeguards. 'Eugenics for general

improvement does not mean trusting the state or any other authority with some arbitrary power for deciding what are good and what are bad hereditary qualities.' At the same time, however, traditional morality is dismissed. 'Anything which permits or promotes open development is right, anything which restricts or frustrates development is wrong. It is a morality of evolutionary direction.'[1] How then can the actual demands of breeding be kept under control? Obviously, if radical changes are to be achieved, extraordinary powers have to be allocated to certain members of society, and the task of breeding men cannot but make those powers inhuman. Nietzsche's demands which were logically correct but humanly repellent should be heeded as a warning.

Nietzsche later understands his own teaching as a terrible warning, and takes the view of it which we have. But before discussing the positive aspect of his work, I want to re-emphasize very strongly its negative aspect, for it should never be forgotten how horrifying, how terrifying his philosophy actually is. He himself recognizes what this philosophy means, and it is this recognition of the true meaning of his own thought which leads him a long way towards the right conclusions, towards developing an attitude very near to that of the later Existentialists. Yet the unqualified praise of Nietzsche by some, especially by French Existentialists, seems to me dangerous, because it may lead—indeed it has led—to an unconscious acceptance of much that is pernicious in his work. It is still of the utmost importance to prevent anyone from falling under the spell of Nietzsche.

CHAPTER III

NIETZSCHE AND EXISTENTIALISM

When we try to understand Nietzsche fully, we are confronted with one great difficulty. We have to try to reconcile not only those occasional contradictions which may occur in any philosophical work, but also many fundamental ones. For instance, when the Pan-German Association of his day, a kind of predecessor of the Nazis, wanted to make him their president, they expected him to be pleased. He disappointed the admirers of his 'blond beast'—who took the 'blond' too literally—by his contemptuous 'definition of the Teuton: obedience and long legs.'[1] A more important example can be seen in his reaction to his sister's marriage to the leader of the then anti-Semitic movement; she expected her brother to be delighted; certainly she could find in his books much to support her expectations. But he warned her that 'your husband's way of thinking is not at all mine', and later wrote to her: 'It is a matter of honour to me to be absolutely honest and unambiguous concerning anti-Semitism—namely to reject it', and complained bitterly that recently he had been more frequently misunderstood because he had become the relative of a well-known anti-Semite.[2] Later the Nazis tried to make him their philosopher, while today Existentialists claim that their interpretation was wrong and that he is really far different; moreover both sides can support their claim with a large number of quotations which they have no need to falsify. But I think we can understand these contradictions if we distinguish between his teaching and his personal development.

We considered his teaching in the last chapter, and shall

now discuss that aspect of his philosophy which mirrors his personal development. This means that we shall concentrate on what is valuable in his philosophy. However, the terrifying implications of what is wrong in it should still be borne in mind, otherwise, as I have emphasized before, his teaching may still prove very dangerous. His personal development leads Nietzsche to a recognition of the dangers of his own teaching and thus beyond it—in fact very near to what today is called Existentialism.

Perhaps the best starting point for discussing the positive aspect of his development is his frequent statement that 'God is dead; we have killed God; God has died.' This is obviously not the statement of a straightforward atheist. The atheist would simply say that there is no God, that belief in him is a nonsensical superstition and has no foundation whatever; but the phrase 'God is dead' refers to the loss of faith. Nietzsche recognizes that Christianity has lost its hold over the majority of the Europeans, especially over the majority of intellectuals, and that this is the most significant event in the nineteenth century, far more important than all the events mentioned in the history books. For, as European civilization had been based on the Christian concept of God, the disappearance of faith must necessarily leave a void at the very heart of our civilization; instead of God there is nothing, *das Nichts*, *Le Néant*. Nietzsche recognizes, too, why this situation is fraught with danger—this sense of emptiness is not static, it grows constantly and destructively, undermining more and more convictions. More and more concepts, values, beliefs, creeds—hitherto the foundations of our lives—crumble and have to be discarded. In the end we are confronted by nothingness as the core of our existence. Such a sense of emptiness is still increasing and threatens to engulf everything of real value which is still left to us.

The recognition of the significance of this process is perhaps

Nietzsche's greatest merit and gives his work prophetic stature. Already in one of his earlier works, he states the problem in an allegorical way. 'Have you not heard of the madman,' he writes, 'who on a bright morning lit a lantern and ran into the market-place, crying incessantly: "I am searching for God?" ... As it happened, many were standing there who did not believe in God, and so he aroused great laughter.' (These are the true atheists to whom this kind of language must appear ridiculous.) 'The madman leapt into their very midst ... "Where is God", he exclaimed, "well, I will tell you. We have killed him—you and I. We, all of us, are his murderers. But how did we do this deed? How did we manage to drink the ocean dry? Who gave us the sponge to wipe away the whole horizon? What were we about when we unchained this earth from its sun? Whither is it moving now? Whither are we moving? Away from all suns? Are we not falling incessantly? Backwards, sideways, forwards, in all directions? Can we still talk about 'above' and 'below'? Are we not wandering, lost, through an infinity of nothingness? ... Is night not approaching, and more and more night? ... God is dead! God remains dead! And we have killed him! What possible comfort is there for us? ... Is not the greatness of the deed too heavy for us?" ' And Nietzsche also knows that this event has not yet been noted; the madman says: 'I have come too early ... This immense event is still on its way ... it has not yet reached the ears of men.'[1] Later, when praising in no uncertain terms the superman in *Thus Spake Zarathustra*, Nietzsche also writes that he foresees something terrible because there is nothing left which is of any value, nothing which commands 'Thou shalt'. In short, he really foresees our present situation.

At the same time, Nietzsche is an honest philosopher and therefore recognizes that the behaviour of the Europeans of his time is fundamentally dishonest. For at this time Napoleon is being worshipped everywhere, in Germany, Italy and Russia just as much as in France where this worship was sufficiently prevalent to bring Napoleon III to the throne. Wars are taken for granted. Darwin's ruthless life and death struggle for survival has, as we have seen, deeply influenced European morality by seeming to justify ruthless competition, ruthless class warfare, ruthless nationalism. Thus, while in their everyday life men disregard most of the Christian commandments, the majority still profess traditional or Christian morality and attend church on Sundays. Does Nietzsche attempt to develop a morality and philosophy which is more in keeping with the actual life of the Europeans of his time? Is it thus that he is led to his praise of vitality, of the ruthless blond beast, to the ideal of the superman? He tries to establish philosophically the superior rights of the strong, which society has conceded already, and he develops his blond beast as an antidote to biological decadence, because the fears of his time seem to call for such a remedy. He faces the logical consequences of a process that has already begun and goes as far as to proclaim: 'What are our cathedrals if not the tombstones of God?'[1]

Initially, Nietzsche certainly believed that his new teaching of the superman could fill the void, that he was providing man with a creed which could replace the old religion. Gradually, however, he realizes that his teaching is not a remedy, but a further contributory force to decadence and destruction; he recognizes it as part of that nihilism which he sees in the making. (We shall discuss his definition of nihilism in a moment.) Yet, despite his knowledge, he forces himself, with the passion of a consistent thinker, to develop his teaching to its final conclusions, so as to demonstrate where it leads; in the end, however, it is no longer meant to be taken as a doctrine, but as a warning. A warning that ruthlessness, wars, controlled breeding with all its consequences, destruction and degradation lie ahead if the convictions which actually dominate life are allowed to work themselves out completely. One could almost say that Nietzsche sacrificed himself to make this warning plain, for his teaching ran utterly contrary to his nature and seems to have contributed to his collapse into insanity. But the word 'sacrifice' must be used with some reservations, for it implies a conscious action, and we cannot be quite sure how far Nietzsche was conscious of what he was doing. For here we are confronted with another difficulty. Nietzsche forced himself to press his teaching to its ultimate conclusions; yet when he had accomplished this self-imposed task, his mental breakdown was imminent, so that there was insufficient time for him to give full expression to his final attitude. We are left with hints and indications.

Nevertheless, some of these indications are clear and unambiguous. In fact, a strange reversal occurs when one gets to know Nietzsche better. At first, the teaching alone is prominent and the claim that there is another side to his philosophy seems rather unconvincing. Yet gradually, as one learns to see the other side and discovers passages contradicting the main trend of his thought even in his early works—such as the story of the madman just quoted—the contradicting statements acquire more and more weight, until, in the end, the 'other' Nietzsche appears as the 'real' one. We discover the moralist who violated himself, so as to be able to adopt an immoral attitude, the over-sensitive man who made himself praise ruthlessness. In this way it also seems more and more likely in the end that he intends his teaching to be a warning, and that he explores this 'immoral' way of life in order to show its consequences, rather than to make the ideas attractive to us.

The main source which points to Nietzsche's change of mind is his unfinished work *The Will to Power*, which was published and edited by his sister. Despite recent research and rearrangement of the material we do not know what Nietzsche himself would have done with this collection of short notes, unfinished remarks and polished, elaborate aphorisms. Some of them obviously belong to an earlier period, some to the years immediately before his breakdown. There is the earlier Nietzsche in the attacks upon Christianity, or when he says that 'not mankind, but the superman is the aim.'[1] He recognizes all the dangers of nihilism, yet he also tries to show it as necessary for a strong life. But there are statements which leave us in no doubt.

Nietzsche now sees his own development clearly. 'Only late in life has one the courage to admit what one actually knows to be true. I have admitted to myself only recently that, until now, I have been a nihilist through and through; the energy and ruthlessness with which I pursued nihilism made me overlook this fundamental fact.'[2] This statement is as unambiguous as one could wish and in no need of further interpretation. At the same time the term 'nihilism' is fully defined. 'What is nihilism? The fact that the highest values lose all value. There is no aim, no answer to the question "Why?" Radical nihilism is the conviction that the highest values which one wants to accept are really untenable, and added to this is the insight that there is no justification whatever for assuming that there is another world or a true nature of things or anything divine or a given morality.'[3] And he adds as 'the clearest symptom of nihilism: Man has lost all his dignity in his own eyes.'[4] This is a valid diagnosis of an illness which is perhaps better known to us than to Nietzsche's own day. For Nietzsche himself, the contemporary situation of man is thus made so clear that he can even add a correct appreciation of Christian morality. 'What advantages did the Christian moral hypothesis offer?' he asks, and answers:

1. It invested man with an absolute value, in contrast to his smallness and accidentalness in the flux of growth and decay.
2. It served the apologists of God, inasmuch as, despite suffering and evil, it allowed the world the attributes of perfection— even that famous 'freedom of will'—evil appeared meaningful.
3. It implanted in man a knowledge of absolute values and thus gave him adequate knowledge precisely where it was most essential.
4. It saved man from self-disgust, from a denial of life, from despairing of knowledge; it was a conserving force.

In summa: Morality was the greatest antidote to practical and theoretical nihilism.[1]

Naturally, Nietzsche does not feel quite at home in this world of Christian morality. His answers are still, at least in part, slightly ironical, and he sees nihilism as a consequence of Christianity. 'Now comes the time when we must pay for the fact that we have been Christians for almost two thousand years'.[2] Yet as the main defect of Christianity he mentions that truthfulness has been made a habit. But is it really a defect, even in his own eyes? It is this very truthfulness which leads him to recognize the nihilism of his teaching.

Another unmistakable sign of Nietzsche's plight is to be found in his most famous book *Thus Spake Zarathustra*. Here, praising it ecstatically, he gives final shape to the ideal of the superman; once this is done, however, the discovery of a new idea is announced with the same ecstasy. This new idea then turns out to be that of 'eternal recurrence', the belief that everything which has ever existed or happened must return again and again unchanged. There is no development, no progress, no possibility of correcting errors, nothing which could make improvement credible; everything is bound to return again and again in exactly the same way. Obviously, this is another fundamental contradiction. Either there is development, and then we might expect a realization of the superman in the future, or there is eternal recurrence, admitting no change whatever, and then the superman must remain eternally impossible. In the book the contradiction is obscured by the ecstatic style, but it must have been obvious to Nietzsche. Nor can we fail to detect its meaning. He forces himself, as we have said, to pursue his thoughts to their ultimate conclusions; but once this has been done, his despair breaks through. In fact, nobody could bear the thought that everything is bound to return without change, that no mistakes could ever be undone, that nobody could ever learn from experience. This, however, is exactly what Nietzsche admits in *The Will to Power*. 'That this exclamation "In vain!" represents the character of our present nihilism is what is to be shown... Duration, combined with this "In vain", without any aim and purpose, is the most paralysing thought... To think it in its most terrifying form: existence, as it is, without meaning or aim, but inevitably returning, without any *finale* in nothingness—"eternal recurrence." This is the most extreme form of nihilism: nothingness (meaninglessness) eternal!'[1]

In another context, Nietzsche writes of this eternal recurrence that he had had the most terrifying thought, and that he then had to create the superman so that there would be one being who could bear this thought. What begins with belief in progress culminates in despair.

It is this insight into the true nature of his own teaching which enables Nietzsche to foresee, to an astonishing extent, certain essential characteristics of the twentieth century. We have mentioned before that he expects it to be 'the classical age of war',* and he also predicts 'compulsory military service with real wars in which all joking is laid aside'[2]—this in the late nineteenth century which knew only such minor wars as that of 1870/71, and when it seemed probable that war would

* See p. 33.

disappear altogether. For Nietzsche, the coming age is one founded on 'the great war, military organization, nationalism, the competition of industry, science and pleasure'; its development will be brought about by 'the right to attack, the power of the appetites, slavery, revenge', and its crowning product will be 'the great criminal'. We have, since his day, witnessed the rise of some such crowning products. Most striking perhaps is his characterization of the nihilist who is to come. 'Not knowing, in the innermost core of his being, whither he is going. Emptiness. The attempt to overcome it by intoxication: intoxication by music, intoxication by cruelty in the tragic enjoyment of the downfall of the noblest men, intoxication by blind worship of single men or ages ... The attempt to submerge oneself in frenzied work, as a tool of science; to open one's eyes to the many small pleasures ... the modesty to generalize about oneself ... some sort of mysticism, a voluptuous enjoyment of the eternal void; Art for Art's sake, "pure" knowledge, as a narcotic against self-disgust, any kind of working routine, any silly little fanaticism; a confusion of all means, illness as a result of a general lack of moderation (excess kills pleasure).'[1] At the same time, Nietzsche knows that nihilism cannot possibly remain a kind of contemplative Buddhism: 'Nihilism is not merely contemplation of this "in vain" and not merely the belief that everything deserves to fall in ruins: one sets oneself to do it, to ruin everything ... This, if you like, is illogical: but the nihilist does not believe in the necessity of being logical ... It is not possible to stop merely at saying "No".'[2]

And the causes of nihilism? There is another series of notes which obviously outlines a longer portion of Nietzsche's unfinished posthumous work—a series which would require and justify detailed consideration.[3] A few remarks must suffice to indicate its scope.

It begins with the question: 'Nihilism is at hand. Where does it come from, this most uncanny of our guests?' and Nietzsche then defines his starting point: 'It is an error to think that social needs or physiological decadence or corruption are the causes of nihilism. Our age is the most honest and sensitive age.' He draws attention to an element in our situation which is really confusing; we are probably more sensitive than previous ages—to war for instance, which was taken for granted until very recently, or to injustice wherever it may occur, and perhaps we are also more honest than, say, the nineteenth century, in dealing with practical affairs and social problems. But this does not help us much, because our awareness of what is wrong is not matched by an equal awareness of what we ought to do.

As actual causes of nihilism Nietzsche enumerates among others:

1. 'The decay of Christianity ... As a reaction against the belief "God is truth" we have now the fanatical belief "Everything is false".' It is remarkable that Nietzsche, previously so critical of Christianity, should now put its weakening first among the causes of nihilism. This 'existential' relevance of Christianity which he probably has in mind will be discussed in the next chapter.

2. 'Scepticism concerning morality is the most decisive fact. After the attempt to escape into a world beyond, the moral interpretation of this world is left without sanctions, and thus the ending is nihilism. Everything has become meaningless.' He accuses the philosophers who tried to abolish the 'moral God' of contributing to this disaster, mentioning especially Hegel (who prepared the way for the belief in progress), and also including Pantheism (which seemed to many to offer an alternative to Christianity). As morality rests upon a belief in the freedom of the will, determinism—in

47

whatever form it may appear—must destroy it. Rather surprisingly, Nietzsche adds as further causes of nihilism in this paragraph: 'The disappearance of the popular ideals of the sage, the saint, the poet'—an indication of the values which he would now like to establish.

3. 'The antagonism between "true" and "beautiful" and "good".' These traditional absolute values present a problem because they are both different and interconnected. They are different because truth refers to the fundamental nature of things, while beauty is shown in their appearance, their external form, and goodness concerns human actions. But that they are also interconnected becomes obvious if one wants to dismiss one of them, for such an attempt always undermines the other as well. Nietzsche was probably thinking of the cult of beauty in his own age (he later mentions Romanticism) which regarded truth and goodness as irrelevant and thus led very often to the kind of superficial sumptuousness which we find, for instance, in Victorian or Wilhelminian architecture. Today beauty is diminished in its value by being considered to be 'merely a matter of taste'; but once this is done, goodness soon becomes merely a matter of taste, too; this we shall discuss in the fifth chapter. Truth, moreover, is thus restricted to scientific truth, which, as we have said before, cannot do justice to the truth to be found in human experience.

4. 'The nihilistic consequences of present-day natural science . . . which finally leads to its turning against itself, to an anti-scientific attitude. Since Copernicus man moves from the centre into x'—into the unknown. Here Nietzsche touches upon a view which is very prominent in Existentialism. While the Age of Reason acclaimed natural science because it revealed the true magnitude of the universe, Pascal was already afraid that infinity and eternity were bound to lose their meaning because the Copernican system transferred them from

the spiritual to the material world. 'When I consider the short
duration of my life, swallowed up in the eternity before and
after, the little space which I fill, and even can see, engulfed
in the infinity of spaces of which I am ignorant, and which
know me not, I am frightened... The eternal silence of these
infinite spaces frightens me.'¹ But Nietzsche also sees the
danger of Existentialism—that the reaction against a purely
scientific attitude may lead many to complete irrationalism.

5. 'The nihilistic consequences of the political and economic
way of thinking, where all principles become mere histrionics'
and which creates 'an atmosphere of mediocrity, miserableness,
insincerity etc.' Later he also refers to 'the nihilistic consequences of history'. We have seen in the first chapter that the
approaches which he attacks cannot enable us to deal with inner
experiences. This is what Nietzsche seems to have in mind, for
he adds, again rather surprisingly: 'We lack the class of men
concerned with salvation, those who could justify us, the man
who saves us'—another astonishing reference to his new values.

6. 'Nationalism'—without any comments. Nietzsche obviously takes it for granted that nationalism establishes wrong
values, a fact which should be borne in mind when fanatical
nationalists of any kind try to make him their philosopher.

There is also a specific reference to Richard Wagner's opera
The Twilight of the Gods. In the old myth, this twilight means
a complete destruction of the divine and human world and
should, therefore, be seen as a disaster. Wagner, however,
romanticizes and idealizes it, which makes Nietzsche call this
opera 'the preparation of nihilism', since it paves the way for
a nihilistic enjoyment of destruction.

The diagnosis of our age, the awareness of nothingness and
of the danger of enjoying nothingness, the rejection of logic—
these aspects of Nietzsche's philosophy prepare the way for
what is to-day called Existentialism, as Sartre acknowledges

when he says: 'The silence of the transcendent, combined with the perseverance of the religious need in modern man, that is the great concern today as yesterday. It is the problem which torments Nietzsche.' But there is also another link with this way of thinking, which Nietzsche himself calls 'experimental thinking'—he not only endeavours to pursue all his ideas to their ultimate conclusions, but also strives to live by them. For him, as for the Existentialists, the task of philosophy is not to erect an abstract system divorced from life as it is actually lived, but to reveal a way of life which can be tested by experience.

We have already mentioned that Nietzsche's teaching is utterly foreign to his own nature. War, which he later praises, was a terrible experience for him, although he took part only in the minor war of the 1870–71 and only as a medical orderly, for as he had become a Swiss citizen by then, he was not allowed to serve as a soldier. The atmosphere of warfare engulfed him like 'gloomy fog'; 'for a time I heard nothing but a sound of wailing which never seemed to end.'[1] When his sister tried to comfort him in his personal conflicts and told him that he 'should be cheerful, for it is a fresh and merry war', he considered this advice, which was quite in keeping with his own ideas, as the bitterest irony and confessed: 'I am badly made for enmity.' He struggles against pity as man's greatest danger because he is completely subject to it. His teaching is worked out at great personal cost: 'I took sides against myself for everything which particularly hurt me and came hard to me.'[2] And he does so because he believes: 'Our defects are the eyes through which we see the ideal.' Without exaggeration he can say of himself: 'We have destroyed the bridge—nay, more, the land—behind us ... Nothing remains but to be courageous, whatever may result from it.'[3]

Nietzsche is one of the few who face the possibility that, instead of becoming a superman, man may deteriorate, may revert to the ape or to some kind of inhuman creature. When he asserts that nothing is true and everything permitted, he exposes himself to the assault of any thought and dares to live without any shelter. It is thus that he comes to demand a philosophical attitude which is essential to Existentialism: 'We must constantly give birth to our thoughts from our pains and, like mothers, give them all that we have within us of blood, heart, fire, lust, passion, torments, conscience, destiny, doom.'[1] Here it becomes obvious that he is indeed willing to sacrifice himself to his philosophy. (We expressed some reservations about such an idea before, but these referred to his degree of awareness of the final stage in his development and not to his attitude in general.) Addressing himself, he leaves no doubt about the scope of his demands: 'You will never again pray, never again worship, never again find peace in an infinite trust—you will never again be able to be at rest before a last wisdom, a last goodness, a last power, and unharness your thought . . . there is for you no longer a divine avenger, one who sets things to rights as a last resort . . . there is no longer any resting place for your heart, where it has only to find and no more to seek.'[2] This is a moving resolve and it indicates both the perils of his teaching and his willingness to suffer.

In the end, he broke down. Though his insanity was probably the outcome of a physical illness, such a breakdown may well have been accelerated by unbearable thoughts. We may assume that thoughts utterly alien to one's nature may contribute to an earlier outbreak of such a disease, and Nietzsche seems to provoke his insanity almost intentionally. Neither of his friends, Peter Gast and Overbeck, can escape the terrifying impression that he fled to madness for refuge, and that he was only pretending to be insane. This we now know to have been wrong, yet, once the last remaining barriers of consciousness were down, it became clear how much of his true nature he had suppressed for so long. When in the streets of Turin he saw a peasant being cruel to a horse, pity overwhelmed him; he embraced it and called it 'brother'—a strange word in Nietzsche's mouth. He signed his last letters, written at the onset of his madness, 'Nietzsche-Caesar', but also 'Dionysos the Crucified'.

His attitude to Jesus is particularly characteristic. His ferocious attacks against Christianity are directed solely against the church: 'The church is precisely that against which Jesus preached—and against which he taught his disciples to preach.'[1] On the whole he attacks that wrong interpretation of Jesus' teaching commonly ascribed to St. Paul, whom he hates as the founder of the church, but he avoids attacking Jesus himself. Even in the book *The Antichrist* Nietzsche hardly touches upon the essentials of Christ's teaching. Instead he calls Jesus a 'psychological type', which may sound derogatory until we discover that he uses the same kind of vocabulary to describe his own character. We realize how just in fact is his understanding of Christ when we find, in *The Will to Power*, the following aphorism: 'If the criminal who is being crucified with Christ and suffering a painful death yet believes that the way in which this Jesus is suffering and dying, without revolt, without feeling enmity, full of love and goodness, simply accepting his death, is the only right way—if these are the criminal's thoughts, then he has understood and accepted the gospel and he has entered paradise.'[2] It is in this book, too, that rather surprisingly he says: 'An exemplary life consists in love and humility; in an overflowing heart which does not exclude the lowliest; in the formal renunciation of the desire to be in the right, to defend oneself, to win a personal triumph.'[3]

At one point he remarks that only Dostoevsky would be able to describe the world of the gospels. This, while showing Nietzsche's perceptiveness, also reminds us of the limitations of his achievements. It was Dostoevsky, first sentenced to death and then reprieved and sent to a labour camp in Siberia, who seemed fated to go mad; yet it was Dostoevsky, the epileptic, the gambler, a man constantly overwhelmed by destructive passions, whose life was extremely hard, who finally attained to that balance of mind and serenity which, with Nietzsche, always remained forced. In fact, Nietzsche prepares the way for Existentialism mainly by his negative criticisms, by the diagnosis of his age, by the destruction of prejudices and by showing the conclusions to which, in contrast to common expectations, many of the accepted beliefs will lead; he does not prepare the way by any positive new teaching. Nietzsche himself could well have been a character in one of Dostoevsky's novels, as at least two of Dostoevsky's characters suggest (Kirillov whom we have already mentioned, and Ivan Karamazov), but Dostoevsky transcends the scope of Nietzsche. In one of his poems Nietzsche expresses his longing for 'the unknown God'; yet despite many profound insights not only God, but any positive answer which could face the challenge of his own destructive criticism eluded him. Traditional morality and Christianity made some impact upon him, but he was only just beginning to recognize their value, and that unwillingly, when, too soon, he became insane. That Existentialist philosophy, despite all its excesses, does contain positive elements is due, not to him, but to Kierkegaard.★

★ I am aware that I have dealt only with two limited aspects of Nietzsche's philosophy, which does not do him full justice. Some of his most penetrating insights— what he says about the positive significance of illness, for instance, or about the nature of the artist, to mention only two—have not even been touched upon. Nevertheless, the statement that his importance lies mainly in his negative achievement seems to me to remain correct in a wider context, too. Again and again he makes brilliant analytical statements which have led others farther along the same path; but the works of these (for instance of Thomas Mann who was deeply influenced by Nietzsche) belong to the end of an epoch and not to the beginning of a new one. Nowhere can I discover a sign that the influence of Nietzsche has contributed directly to such a new beginning. However, indications of a new development of ideas have since been shown; see especially chapter VIII.

Destructive as Nietzsche's philosophy may be, however, it nevertheless makes development possible, because he never bars the way to the future. Honesty means to him to be concerned with 'immanence', to believe only in what can be experienced here and now; he tries to dismiss anything transcendental or supernatural. 'The world of appearances is the only world; the "true world" is a lie added to it.'[1] His philosophy has this approach in common with many others of his time, especially with those which are based on the theory of evolution or other scientific hypotheses; but while most philosophers believe that they are demonstrating that everything can be explained rationally, Nietzsche remains aware that, despite all the problems which may be solved, the fact of existence still represents an insoluble mystery. Because he knows the sense of emptiness created by the disappearance of the Christian concept of God, he also knows that most concepts we use have lost much of their meaning; he therefore tries to re-think all our thoughts in terms of immanence. In this context, however, the many contradictions in his philosophy prove their worth, for they show that none of the new terms can completely replace the transcendental; his clearsightedness and honesty save him from false completeness. Man as god still cannot explain his origin, nor understand his destiny, nor master the universe. Instead, he is plunged into despair. From Nietzsche, we learn to understand why Kierkegaard had earlier made despair the starting point of his positive philosophy of existence.

CHAPTER IV

KIERKEGAARD

When Kierkegaard died, in 1855, it seemed highly improbable that his work would survive. His books were written in Danish, a language rarely known outside his own country, and he was completely unknown except in Denmark itself where he was a popular figure, but even there he was known for reasons which had little to do with his works—his attack on the established church and other personal matters to which we shall refer later. But today, more than a hundred years after his death, we can say without exaggeration that he is one of the most important philosophers and theologians—if not the most important—for our time. The magnitude of his influence upon recent philosophical and theological thinking leads us to the conclusion that his philosophy must have a particular significance for us just at the present moment.

We have mentioned before that it was he who coined the term 'Existentialism'.* The attempts of philosophers to create abstract metaphysical systems reached their culmination at the beginning of the nineteenth century; Kierkegaard opposed all such attempts, attacking especially Hegel, since it was he who claimed to have found a full explanation of everything, of the universe and man, by his reasoning. Kierkegaard insisted that philosophy should not be abstract, but based on personal experience, on the historical situation in which man finds himself, so that it could become the basis, not of speculation, but of each man's life. The only evidence to be accepted was that which both could be and had been tested by experience.

* See pp. 10–11.

Thanks to this approach Kierkegaard understood better than most philosophers one of our main problems—the difficulty modern man faces when he wants to accept a religious belief, in particular Christianity. Perhaps we are no longer so exclusively dominated by scientific ways of thought as the generations before the first World War; there seems to be a great longing for a return to faith. But the difficulty of accepting such faith is still with us and probably, just because of this longing, is even more acutely felt. How can we believe in a transcendental reality in the face of the totally different categories of science and of the successes of materialism; how can we believe in the divine when we are faced with immense suffering and injustice in the world, when we have seen two great wars and the inhuman excesses of totalitarianism? Has it not been said that the existence of even a single lethal bacteria makes belief in a God of Love impossible? Undoubtedly, both the scientific view—which seems to provide a different explanation of the world of its own—and the course of history have made the problem of faith more complex than it ever was before.

To deal with this problem, Kierkegaard tries to understand what faith means in terms of personal experience, and he chooses two biblical figures—Job and Abraham—to help him. In his attempt to understand these two figures he arrives at a deeper vision of faith and sees that it is not an easy consolation but 'fear and trembling'. This enables him to make clear three of the main ideas of Existentialism—the 'absolute paradox', the concept of dread (for which, to emphasize its special meaning, one often uses the German word 'Angst'), and the idea of the 'jump into the abyss', the leap into the unknown.

He presents to us Job, robbed, for no apparent reason, of everything, in utter misery. When Kierkegaard addresses him we feel at once that he is talking to an individual man, not to a conventional figure of tradition, for he says: 'Thee I have need of, a man who knows how to complain aloud, so that his complaint echoes in heaven where God confers with Satan in devising schemes against man.'[1] In this scheming, however, Kierkegaard discerns what determines the situation of each one of us: 'Where am I? Who am I? Who is it that has lured me into the world and now leaves me there? Why was I not consulted?... How did I obtain an interest in this big enterprise they call reality? Why should I have an interest in it? Is it not a voluntary concern? [Why am I] compelled to take part in it?'[2] This almost repeats one of Pascal's cries: 'I am frightened, and am astonished at being here rather than there; for there is no reason why here rather than there, why now rather than then. Who has put me here? By whose order and direction have this place and time been allotted to me?'[3] How can I be held responsible if my birth—and with it my character—are due to a senseless accident?

The emphasis on the enigmatic character of birth (and also of death, as we shall see later) is common to most Existentialists; it is in this way that they constantly keep us aware of how much of our existence must remain a mystery to us, and prevent us from falsifying or oversimplifying our lives by disregarding what cannot be explained. Nobody will ever be able to explain to me why I am born into one nation and age rather than another; into a family not of my choosing, with the character I have rather than a different one which I might much prefer. Some elements of a biological, psychological or social explanation can be adduced, but they are linked to more fundamental causes which remain beyond our grasp. Once this fundamental problem is faced, the answer of philosophy—if there is one—cannot be facile. Kierkegaard is led by it to discover the meaning of faith.

Job's friends try to console him: his suffering is a just

retribution, a punishment for his sins; if he submits to it all will again be well. But Job is not to be consoled so simply, for he knows that this explanation is untrue. He is driven to utter despair because he feels himself in the right even against God: 'The secret in Job, the vital power, the nerve, the idea, is that in spite of everything Job is in the right ... He claims to be on good terms with God, he knows that he is innocent and pure in his inmost heart, where he is conscious that God knows it too, and yet the whole of existence contradicts him.'¹ Yet by this absolute paradox—that he knows he is in the right, even against God, against whom he cannot be right, while the whole of existence contradicts him—he discovers, in his despair, in his fundamental *Angst*, what faith demands, and why, in the last resort, he is nevertheless in the wrong. God is so infinitely greater than man that we cannot hope to understand him fully and thus we must accept the apparently senseless. Job has to praise God for everything, even for the creation of such apparently purposeless creatures as the hippopotamus and the crocodile. Faith means complete surrender; 'to make the movements of faith, [I must] shut my eyes and plunge confidently into the absurd.'² I must take the risk of jumping into the abyss.

The meaning of the 'movements' involved in the act of faith, and the act itself, are further elucidated by the story of Abraham. For Kierkegaard, this, too, is no conventionally elevating story; he tries to re-live Abraham's 'existential situation'. There is God's promise that 'in his seed all races of the world would be blessed ... time passed, it [the promise] became unreasonable, Abraham continued to believe'.³ When very old, an only son was born to him, but then he was asked to sacrifice that son. 'So all was lost—more dreadfully than if it had never come to pass! So the Lord was only making sport of Abraham! He made miraculously the preposterous actual, and now in turn He would annihilate it . . . Who then is He that plucks away the old man's staff . . . Who is He that would make a man's grey hairs comfortless, who is it that requires that he himself shall do it? Is there no compassion for the venerable old man, none for the innocent child? And yet Abraham was God's elect, and it was the Lord who imposed the trial. All would now be lost.'[1] This despair has to be endured; Abraham could not cut it short, by making the sacrifice immediately; for three seemingly endless days and nights he had to journey to the mountain where the sacrifice was to take place. Kierkegaard makes us feel the agony of this long journey; then he describes, in a moving and terrifying way, the last moments of the testing—the collecting of the wood, the sharpening of the knife, the torture of the last seconds before the miracle. Fear and trembling, dread and terror indeed! Yet there is once more the absolute paradox, including the opposite feelings of hope and trust, in spite of all evidence to the contrary; in his inmost heart Abraham must have complete trust—the trust that all will be well, that the senseless will make sense, for it is God who demands the killing of his son. Without this trust, Abraham could not obey, for then the killing of his son would be murder. But the paradox must remain paradoxical to the end: Abraham cannot talk about his trust, not even to himself, for this would make the sacrifice a sham; he has to experience the contradiction between the terrifying demand and the final succour* as insoluble, so that he fully experiences both terror and hope. The hope can only be felt and not expressed. The act of faith— the constantly renewed willingness to believe, to accept and to surrender, despite apparent evidence to the contrary— cannot be made superfluous by unambiguous logical conclusions.

* These are the words of H. H. Farmer who sees God as making us experience an 'absolute demand' and 'final succour'.

Kierkegaard's concept of dread, therefore, is not a matter of understandable and specific fears, nor fears of a danger which can be withstood, but the feeling that the ground beneath one's feet has given way, that all security and certainty have gone, and that not even God can be trusted any longer—'All would now be lost.' When the very foundations of everything by which man lives have been shaken by this fundamental, this metaphysical, kind of dread, then—and only then, according to Kierkegaard—will man discover and fully experience that deeper reality within him with which religion claims to deal. At the same time, the absolute paradox ensures that he cannot seek an easy short cut, but must go on towards the 'jump into the abyss', into the depths of the gulf which separates man from God who, to be God, must utterly transcend the scope of human knowledge.

The paradoxical nature of the situation, however, implies that despite dread and suffering—even, perhaps, because of them—we can be rescued by experiences which counteract them if only we are willing to accept the paradox fully. It is impossible to force faith upon another, we cannot even force it upon ourselves, however passionately we may long for it; but we *can* take the risk of the leap, we are not, whatever our situation, completely powerless. We may be frightened, for the element of paradox makes it obvious that any choice involves a painful risk. However, the decision to make the jump will also be reinforced because, since the paradox cannot be resolved by any abstract and generally valid conclusion, we shall realize that the choice can only be made by ourselves as individuals, that each one of us must make it and experience it himself. 'Either there is the paradox that the individual stands in an absolute relation to the absolute, or Abraham is lost.'[1] Despite the wild improbability that, viewed on the cosmic scale, each infinitesimally small individual matters, man can experience an absoluteness which relates him to the absoluteness of God. The indispensability of the paradox ensures that the leap remains a risk, for, as the glimpse of a positive experience is only confirmed by the consequences of the leap, we can never know beforehand that we are right. But just because it remains a risk, we are exposed to that fullness and depth of experience which is necessary if our metaphysical dread is to be conquered. We shall jump, Kierkegaard believes, 'into the open arms of God.'

Kierkegaard has been accused of making an unwarranted attack on reason by his insistence on the paradox. It is true that he calls it 'a paradox which no thought can master, because faith begins precisely where thinking leaves off.'[1] There is some truth in other criticisms, too. It may be true that he overemphasizes the gulf which separates man from God, thus apparently implying that no spark of the divine exists in man—that man's freedom, as Augustine claimed, is only the freedom to sin, while everything positive emanates from God. But why should we want to take the risk of the jump, if there were no such spark within us? All these criticisms, however, though justified in part—we shall return to some of them later —are not wholly correct, for they ignore the very paradox they attack. Kierkegaard uses reason and the intellect to the utmost, so as to make sure that the irrational does not intrude too early; he only admits it where it cannot be avoided, and reason can no longer help. The experience of dread has to be a shattering experience of complete uncertainty or nothingness, but this is not depressing, for it is thus that the positive within man is disclosed. Kierkegaard's philosophy is undoubtedly austere, perhaps too austere; yet this austerity must not be confused with pessimism, for he believes that, if a man is destroyed by despair, he has not experienced it deeply enough; if he had, he would have discovered, in the innermost depth of his being, a reality which could have saved him. Perhaps we can even say that history has confirmed Kierkegaard's trust in the paradox. He never made Christianity appear easy; he represented faith, not as a consolation or an embellishment of life, but in all its seriousness, as a 'terrifying demand'; and yet it was he—and not those who tried to smooth the way—who did most to reinstate Christianity on the European intellectual scene. His apparently disheartening demands have not proved discouraging, because they restored to Christianity that vigour and majesty which Nietzsche found lacking.

Kierkegaard is mainly preoccupied with his ever-recurring question 'What does it mean to be a Christian?', but the general philosophical importance of his approach is obvious. The absolute paradox throws into relief the limitations of reason, of external knowledge, and points to the need for a different kind of thinking, different from purely logical and scientific—to a way of thinking based on inner participation which we have mentioned in the first chapter and shall later discuss in greater detail. Kierkegaard calls it the 'subjective method'. He applies both the paradox and this method to ethics, too, and here its relevance to philosophy can be even more clearly seen.

Confronted with Abraham's willingness to kill his son, which is immoral and yet justified, Kierkegaard asks: 'Is there such a thing as a teleological suspension of the ethical?'[1] Can the ethical ever be suspended for the sake of a higher purpose, even the most sublime? He does not ask the question light-heartedly; the ethical was, for many years, his prime concern. But here too he discovers the paradox by introducing the concept of sin, and this helps him to find a satisfactory answer.

Ethics deals with moral values and commandments, with good and evil, right and wrong, not with sin, the difference being that moral values are defined either by absolute or

relative moral laws, while sin is an offence against a transcendental reality. But the two concepts—ethics and sin—
can hardly be separated completely; an evil deed is a sin, a
wrongdoer a sinner. Therefore 'an ethics which disregards sin
is a perfectly idle science; but if it asserts sin, it is *eo ipso* beyond
itself'. There is also the confusing contradiction that the moral
law which is a positive, universal principle, should stand
higher than the conception of sin which is a negative, individual
action. But personal experience proves the opposite, for 'by
sin the individual is already higher than the universal', since
he is acting against—and thus in contact with—the transcendental. However, it is once more the contradiction as such
which provides the answer; 'when the individual by his guilt
has gone outside the universal, he can return to it only by
virtue of having come as the individual into an absolute
relationship with the absolute'.[1] By trespassing against the
absolute, the sinner has touched that deeper reality which
can transform him, because he has also touched the source of
forgiveness. God can suspend the ethical, not only in His own
demand to Abraham, but also when a wrong is truly experienced as sin, for this experience involves desperate remorse
and thus leads towards a reconciliation which transcends
ethics.

Does this not reduce, or even deny, the importance of
ethics? Kierkegaard wants to enhance it, but he constantly
shows that ethical demands are so absolute that no mortal
can be perfect enough to fulfil them, that they only make us
profoundly aware of the fact that we are sinners. What then is
the use of a moral law or ethics? Again the paradox has
positive implications. Three things are achieved by it.

First, ethics is seen to be indispensable, for we could not,
without it, achieve full awareness of our state, of the fact
that we are sinners. But, because of the need for this awareness,

ethics does not simply mean a command to obey the moral law; it demands personal participation. Everyone knows how dangerous it is to obey moral rules only for the sake of the rules; unimpeachable behaviour can easily hide such dubious motives as acquiring a good reputation; our virtues can become the meeting places of our vices. The Pharisees, despite their piety, have become a byword for such an attitude. Therefore, to understand ethics, we have to approach it from within and apply the 'subjective method'.

Second, if we do so, we soon discover that the moral law is absolute and not relative, for it cannot be tampered with. We may disregard or disobey it, but we shall still know that we ought to act differently. Sin will be felt to be sin, even if it is denied. Kierkegaard takes as an example the commandment 'Thou shalt love thy neighbour as thyself'—any true relationship with another person makes us know by experience that we ought to treat him in the light of this commandment, even if we do not want to do so or feel unable to. We know for certain that our behaviour ought to be dictated by love, but we may—perhaps we always do—fall short of acting upon this knowledge.

Therefore, Kierkegaard feels entitled to speak, finally, not simply of man's self, but of his 'ethical self'. Morality can only be absolute because it is so deeply ingrained in man that it must be considered as characteristic of his true nature. Man is not, as some Existentialists claim, an undefined being who can be transformed at will, but a moral being.

These moral questions are so essential that we shall discuss them in more detail as well as possible objections against them in a separate chapter. But these few indications should suffice to show that Kierkegaard, far from reducing the status of ethics, gives it on the contrary the greatest possible significance. Just because he sees the limitations of ethics, he succeeds in showing its absoluteness; the knowledge that ethics is built upon religious foundations does not make its laws relative (which, after all, means dependent on something else), but, paradoxically, prevents it from degenerating into relativity. Dependence on something higher than himself, on something absolute, sets man free.

Frequently, the opposite view is held—that the dependence on God, too, makes ethics relative. This would not be Kierkegaard's way of arguing. Freedom obviously means acting in complete agreement with one's innermost nature, without any compulsion foreign to it, and according to Kierkegaard, man's innermost nature is his ethical self. God's appeal to this self, therefore, does not constitute an external compulsion, but sets man free by enabling him to act according to his true nature, and just because the demand is absolute, it sets him absolutely free.*

These assertions, like all references to religion, are based on an act of faith and may sound unconvincing. We shall try, as I have said, to scrutinize them at greater length, paying particular attention to their possible refutation. Kierkegaard makes them convincing by developing them, thus proving the fruitfulness of this approach to ethics, as well as that of the existentialist attitude. This becomes apparent in many of his works, but especially in his book *Works of Love*, in which he discusses word by word the commandment 'Thou shalt love thy neighbour as thyself'. We can give here only a short summary of this lengthy book, which cannot possibly do it justice; but even a brief paraphrase of his commentary on each word will show the wealth of ideas which has been made accessible by the acceptance of the absoluteness of morality.

Thou. The commandment is addressed to me, not to someone else. And it is unconditional—which means that it is not

---

* This line of argument also forms the basis of the conclusions in the next chapter.

simply meant to help me to behave well as far as possible, but that I am asked to begin, regardless of the conditions. To begin to make the good real. Naturally enough I shall be inclined to think that I am an unimportant person, without any noticeable influence, that I can do very little except behave reasonably well, and even that only within limits. Let greater, more powerful men begin, those who are responsible for the government, for large organizations; I can only wait and see what the others are doing and perhaps support them. But Kierkegaard insists that it is my turn to make a start, and that this start is of significance even in the widest context. This may sound unrealistic and therefore impossible—but is it in fact unrealistic?

Under the influence of natural science we have come to believe that an effect can be easily related to its cause. This may no longer apply in modern physics, but as yet these latest developments have hardly affected our way of thinking. In any case, it is certainly not true that the relation between cause and effect can be easily detected in human affairs. Let us consider a few examples which support Kierkegaard's conviction. Imagine a Roman at the time of Jesus saying that this powerless rabbi in a remote corner of the empire, followed by a handful of disciples, represented a greater danger to the existing form and creed of the empire than all men in positions of power; all Rome would have laughed at him. Yet it was exactly this which proved to be true, and in a comparatively short time. Or imagine a Londoner of the 1860's saying that one of these strange foreign refugees, Karl Marx by name, living in great poverty and almost in isolation, was writing a book which would transform the world within a few decades —nobody outside the small inner circle of convinced socialists could possibly have believed him. Or, to give a thoroughly sinister example, in 1921 seven cranks met together in Munich, in a beer cellar of all places, to found the National Socialist party: who would, who could have believed that, at that meeting, the most powerful political party Germany was ever to know was being born? For good and ill, there are mysterious and unforeseeable effects in human history, caused by apparently powerless individuals, whose actions initiate new developments; they can succeed, however, only because there are small groups of equally powerless individuals who are prepared for something new. The individual matters.

In other words: we should be prepared to do things once we know them to be right, once we are convinced that they ought to be done, without speculating overmuch about their chances of success, for these, in a wider context, cannot be foreseen. It is more realistic to obey the commandment unconditionally than to dwell upon the probability or improbability of the desired effect. For instance, what but our convictions of right and wrong can guide us in complex situations, such as those concerned with the existence of atomic weapons, when the arguments on both sides remain so inconclusive?

Our experience will prove that Kierkegaard's approach is justified. Waiting for others to begin is paralysing; it is only by trying to do something that our potentialities are developed. In the attempt, we ourselves become real.

Thou shalt. The commandment is not an appeal to our inclinations; we are told about a duty. But is this not again a paradox? Love, if it is to be genuine, must be spontaneous; everyone knows how dubious the result may be if we force ourselves to try to love a person whom we dislike. And yet, to love one's neighbour is a commandment.

In the fact that love can be made a duty Kierkegaard sees the breaking into our existence of the transcendental. We are, all of us, undoubtedly able to love. There is no excuse: 'Love is not like art ... poured out only on the few' who are

endowed for it; 'everyone who wishes to have love, to him
it is given.'¹ This it already shares with religion; it does not
require any special gifts, it is not restricted to great genius, it is
within reach of everyone.* Love is also independent of external circumstances: 'If someone has cut my hands off,
I cannot play the zither, and if someone has cut my leg off,
I cannot dance . . . and if I myself lie with a broken arm or leg,
then I cannot rush into the flames to save another's life: but I
can be compassionate everywhere.'² Yet the commandment
presupposes even more; it commands an emotion which
should be spontaneous. Therefore, only a love greater than ours,
a love which kindles love within us, can give sense to the
commandment: 'In earthly love and friendship partiality is
the middle term. In love to the neighbour God is the middle
term; if you love God above all else, then you also love your
neighbour and in your neighbour every man.'³

Are we then confronted once more with one of those
religious statements which only become acceptable by an
act of faith? Not entirely, for it is the particular significance of
this commandment that it, in its turn, makes the religious
statement accessible in terms of human experience. For, if we
observe our own reactions when we meet another person
without reservations, we know for certain, as we have
mentioned before, that the commandment is valid.† Morality
has often been called that side of religion which can be discussed; Kierkegaard makes us actually aware, with the help of
logic and reason, that we are citizens of two worlds—of the
human and of the divine. The more so as his discussion of the
word 'neighbour' enlarges that part of human understanding
which looks towards the divine.

* Genius, Kierkegaard insists, is not a religious term, because it is restricted to the
few, and even the founders of the great religions must not be called geniuses, because
their achievements are based on what is common to humanity.

† See p. 64, and chapter V.

Love. Kierkegaard shows that the commandment refers to feeling, not to abstract knowledge. He elaborates Pascal's assertion: 'The knowledge of God is very far from the love of Him', emphasizing like Pascal 'the reasons of the heart.'[1] But just because it is a feeling, it has to be carefully defined; it is not an emotion, be it slight or violent, felt upon a special occasion, such as falling in love; it must be constant and of the right kind, passionate and yet controlled.

Our language is very poor once we try to discuss the more fundamental feelings, especially when we try to elucidate the word 'love'. There have been attempts to establish at least some fundamental distinctions, the two concepts 'love' and 'charity' could be of help if only 'charity' had not changed its meaning to such an extent. Some writers have resorted to the Greek 'agape', but this word has not taken root. Yet even if there were two adequate words to distinguish the love between man and woman from the love of God and of one's neighbour, each word would still have to be used for a variety of very different feelings—such as (to give only a few examples) falling in love, love between husband and wife, between parents and children, between friends; for love of God, of mankind, of single persons as 'neighbours', of an enemy, not to mention other kinds of love such as that of one's country, of beauty or of one's work.[2] It is therefore of particular value that Kierkegaard should succeed in making the meaning of the love of one's neighbour clear by making a wealth of distinctions.

The value of these distinctions depends so much on details that they cannot be reproduced briefly. Some of the quotations used in the discussion of 'Thou shalt' may have given some idea of the direction in which this clarification moves. A humorous remark of Dostoevsky's may serve as a short cut to elucidate it further. In one of his letters he says that it is easy to love the whole of mankind, but that this is not what is required; to be forced to live together in a small room with a stranger whom one cannot stand, who gets on one's nerves, and yet love him—this is what matters. Or, as Dostoevsky also says: 'Everyone can love occasionally, even the wicked can . . . Love in action is a harsh and dreadful thing compared with love in dreams . . . is labour and fortitude.'¹ Such a description of love may sound harsh indeed, but both Kierkegaard and Dostoevsky succeed in making us understand a love which transcends our inclination and moves us to pain by its intensity.

Thy neighbour. Kierkegaard's assertions again sound very austere. 'If you do not see your neighbour so close at hand that you see him . . . unconditionally in every man, then you do not see him at all . . . I love God by how much I love that neighbour to whom by natural inclination I am least drawn.' But the emphasis here is on equality: 'Your neighbour is your equal . . . for with your neighbour you have human equality before God . . . every man unconditionally has this equality, and has it unconditionally.'² It is this equality, however, which gives to the apparent austerity great human warmth.

Let me choose this time an example from Kierkegaard's political views. Disappointed by the revolution of 1848, he seems to be driven towards an ultra-conservative attitude, and what he says may once more appear utopian and unrealistic; but gradually we realize that his way is actually the only one which does full justice to experience. It is a way which gives real life to Christianity, though it makes it a tremendous task at the same time.

As a starting point, he takes the ideals of the French revolution—liberty, equality, fraternity. These ideals were meant originally to abolish differences. But can differences be abolished? 'As little as the Christian lives or can live without a physical body, just as little can he live outside the differences of earthly life to which every individual by birth, by conditions, by circumstances, by education and so on, specially belongs... These differences must continue as long as the temporal existence continues, and must continue to tempt every man who comes into the world'[1]—and they must be increased by liberty. All revolutions which aimed at liberty, therefore, have, as Kierkegaard knew from experience, destroyed equality, while the struggle for equality, as he foresaw (and as we since know from experience), will destroy liberty. The correct starting point, therefore, would be fraternity—that is, love of one's neighbour. But is this possible? Kierkegaard indicates the one condition which would make it possible: man's concentration on his true self. He says:

'Christianity has not wished to storm forth to abolish the differences, neither those of distinction nor of humbleness... but it wants the differences to hang loosely on the individual, loosely, like the cape the king casts off to reveal himself, loosely, like the ragged cloak in which a supernatural being has concealed itself. When the difference hangs thus loosely, then that essential other is always glimpsed in every individual, that common to all, that eternal resemblance, the equality.'[2]

Here we feel Kierkegaard's great humility and compassion, and the metaphor of the cape the king casts off, of the ragged cloak in which Christ conceals himself, is not only very beautiful, but also strikingly to the point—in a flash of insight we do see the right attitude. The fundamental equality of all men explains the word 'neighbour'; only because of it can love be commanded; only by its acceptance can we obey the commandment. Kierkegaard, however, also ensures that this attitude is not sentimentalized, by again including ethics as well. He goes on: Christianity 'has never in an external sense striven for a place in the world of which it is no part, and yet it has infinitely changed everything...It transforms every relationship between man and man into a conscience-relationship.' This puts us firmly on human ground. As, however, this equality cannot be discerned from outside, because from outside we see only the differences, we have to be subjective to recognize it. We need to learn 'inwardness'—to consider these relationships from inside.

As Thyself. As we ourselves participate in this fundamental equality, man's duty to himself is the same as that to his neighbour; but it must be safeguarded against distortion; it must become neither self-obsession nor selfishness. This is achieved because the commandment is reciprocal. If I love myself as my neighbour I shall respect in myself the same humanity—if I love him as myself it is impossible for me to remain impersonal or detached. We are led towards the right kind of subjectivity which Kierkegaard clarifies by an elaboration of the subjective method. This is his direct contribution to philosophy, and to it we must turn.

But first, to enable us to judge it properly, we must discuss more fully the absoluteness of morality which, in this chapter, we have taken for granted.

CHAPTER V

MORALITY—RELATIVE OR ABSOLUTE?

In this book, the word 'morality' is not used in its superficial or colloquial sense, referring to some kind of custom, but in its original, fundamental meaning. It could be defined as a pattern of behaviour based on the absolute value of the good. This definition, however, confronts us immediately with the problem I wish to discuss now—is there really a morality which can be considered as absolute? If there is, it would mean that there is a morality which is not simply the result of social, psychological or other factors, but which is independent of anything else, an ultimate fact, the embodiment of an absolute value—that is, of an intrinsic value which must be accepted as such, because it cannot be derived from any other, more basic principle. Can we really assume that such a morality exists?

To ask this question raises another which must be answered first. In which way is it possible to discuss absoluteness? We are moving here in the sphere of convictions and judgments where material or scientific proofs do not apply. We have to rely on inner experience; yet many people—perhaps the majority today—believe that morality is not absolute, but continually changing under the influence of various and varying conventions. Certainly, the social fabric seems to be undermined by the lack of absolute standards, but that these standards appear desirable is not a sufficient reason to make them real. We can accept them only if we are fully convinced that they do in fact exist. However, as the word 'absolute' means underived, ultimate, beyond proof, it seems to preclude any further discussion.

Nevertheless, there are two ways in which such a discussion can be fruitfully conducted. First, one can set out what absolute morality means and implies, and trust that the assumption, if it is correct, will awaken in the experience of everyone a response which confirms its existence. This is the method we have used in the preceding chapter. Second, we can scrutinize those theories—or at least some of the most important ones—which deny the absoluteness of morality and consider it is relative, as the product of more basic factors, in order to find out whether such theories can be accepted as the whole truth, or whether they involve omissions. If we find omissions, however, we can also try to see whether the elements lacking in any such explanation could be accounted for by the claim that there is an absolute morality. This is the procedure which I propose to follow in this chapter.

For this purpose, we have to introduce a further qualification of the term 'morality'. It is not to be understood as establishing rules for every single occasion, which would demand an adaption to these occasions and thus make it relative, but as a fundamental law which we find ourselves unable to deny and which, therefore, can guide us in different circumstances. Thus we must also distinguish between the moral law as such and its application; the assertion that morality is relative is often based on a confusion between the two. For instance, in any such discussion the objection is invariably made that the Christian religion allows only one wife, whereas the Moslem religion allows four, which seems to prove that morality depends on conventions. However, the question of the number of wives does not belong to morality in the sense in which we want to use the word; it is only when we ask how the husband behaves to his wife or wives that the realm of true morality has been entered. We are concerned neither with the application of morals, which naturally depends on external conditions, nor with men's failure to live according to their convictions, but with morality itself.

To make the discussion of this basic morality possible, the main principle of Existentialism has to be applied—experience has to be admitted as evidence. We have, as honestly as we possibly can, to test any assertion about morality in the light of our own experience. In the last resort, such a test must remain subjective—that is, it must be influenced by what is characteristic of our own personalities. But there are a few considerations which we can keep in mind and thereby ensure that we are not unduly influenced by our individual inclinations or prejudices—considerations which help us to develop the 'subjective method' and thus to reveal those aspects of our personality which, as basic characteristics of humanity, are shared by all men.

1. When confronted with theories about morality, we should ask the question: 'Do I really recognize myself in these theories?' All such theories claim to deal with facts which I am supposed to experience within myself; to think of my actual experience will help me to avoid those abstract speculations which falsify my views and thus gradually affect my further experience also. We have mentioned how deeply man is influenced by the ideas he has about himself;* to ask this question is therefore essential.

That the question is justified can be seen when we compare the possibility of discussing morality with that of discussing religion. Morality, as we have said, is often called that side of religion which can be discussed†—which means that it can be discussed without reference to religion. When I state a moral commandment correctly—such as 'Thou shalt love thy

* See p. 23.   † See p. 68.

neighbour as thyself'—I may hope that every person, even if he dislikes it or seems to reject it, will respond and realize, in his innermost being, that the commandment is valid. No such common response can be expected to religious statements; as faith requires an act of faith, even the claim that God exists may, without this act, remain meaningless. This difference between morality and religion probably explains why the moral demands of the great religions—of Judaism, Christianity, Buddhism, Confucianism, Taoism—are very similar, while the religions themselves differ considerably. Both morality and religion transcend the region of material proofs, but only with morality am I entitled to assume that my own experiences, if properly formulated and tested, apply to everybody, that they convey a knowledge of general validity. A discussion of religion would have to be conducted in a less direct way; with morality, the direct question is called for.

2. The final version of Kant's Categorical Imperative—'Act so that you use humanity, in your own person as well as in any other, always as an end, and never as means only'[1]—provides us with another test.

This test is particularly important in our complicated society where it is often inevitable that men should be treated in certain contexts—in a census of population, for instance, or as producers of goods—as units and means. This, however, is done too frequently and almost as a matter of course, regardless of whether man's humanity is involved (it cannot, after all, be easily excluded); we must therefore constantly remind ourselves that to treat man as means only is fundamentally wrong. This will help us to recognize not only where we ourselves go wrong, but also where others or where theories about morality do.

The imperative also implies that the maxim 'The end

justifies the means' is basically immoral. Again, we cannot altogether avoid acting according to it; occasionally, as when we tell a lie so as not to cause suffering, it may even lead to a good action. Nevertheless, from the purely moral point of view not even the loftiest end can justify evil means; evil remains evil, whatever its purpose. If we consult experience, we can see from a practical point of view why this is so. The means are what we actually experience and so we are fashioned by them; the end is far away and may never be reached, so that it may well remain immaterial for our actions. Thus the means will prove stronger than the end; if they are bad, they will spoil even the best ends. Human imperfection may force us to choose the lesser of two evils, but only if we remain aware of the fact that they are evils can we hope to restore morality.

3. The distinction between 'good' and 'right' will be of further help and will further clarify the last point. The distinction cannot be established once and for all, because both concepts can be defined only in special cases and not in general. Yet in special cases their difference is clear. It may be right to punish a child; but is it also good? Many people say that it is right to hang a murderer, but few would claim that the hanging itself is a good act. On the other hand, it may be good, as we have just mentioned, to tell a lie instead of making somebody suffer; but it is not wholly right.

To become conscious of this tension between what is good and what is right will increase our sensitivity and sharpen our awareness, and this is, in the sphere of values, of the utmost importance. There we do not find clear-cut rules and definitions which could be applied to every occasion; we shall see that even conflicting loyalties—between the demands of one's family and the duty to one's country, for instance—cannot be avoided. But I have to come to my own conclusions and to make my own decisions; I act morally only if I do what is good because I myself recognize it to be good. Therefore I have to develop my sense of values, and all clearer distinctions will contribute to this end. It is not the definition which matters, but the clarification of my immediate reaction in a particular situation.

4. We ought to be aware of what we are rejecting if we dismiss absolute morality. It cannot be separated from the freedom of the will—the freedom of choice, decision, action—and the one cannot be denied without calling the others in question. If we are not free to decide, however, we are not responsible—that is, responsibility disappears and conscience loses its significance. Thus the basis of trust between persons is lost. The concepts 'good' and 'evil' lose their full meaning; as they no longer determine actions, they become virtually quasi-aesthetic terms—that is, the discussion of morality is replaced by a discussion of preferences, of an arbitrary pattern of choices, of detached judgments, all of which do not establish obligations. The statement 'this action is good' then means no more than 'I like this action'—as one might say 'I like this landscape'—and all discussion of morality becomes meaningless.

We have said before that the desirability of absolute morality is no proof of its existence; but to know the consequences of its rejection will give to our decision about the nature of morality that weight which such a decision requires.

Bearing these considerations in mind, let us now turn to the discussion of some of the theories which try to establish that morality is relative—that is, dependent on something else. To avoid any misunderstanding, however, I should like to emphasize that I do not want to reject all these theories in their entirety; some of them contain elements which can be justified and are important; they can help us to distinguish what is in fact moral from what is not. I am concerned with the question whether or not these theories leave out some aspects of morality, thus indicating a gap in which the absolute seems in place.

The least important of these theories is the biological one. For present-day biology, the criterion is the fitness to survive; morality, therefore, far from being absolute or dictated by conscience, is seen as a means, developed by natural selection, to increase this fitness—for instance, by developing the herd-instinct. Yet even within the herd natural selection chooses the strongest individuals; moral man would thus have to be, in a biological sense, the stronger man. Morality, however, is in many respects dangerous to survival. To love one's enemy, or to offer the other cheek, are undoubtedly among the highest moral demands, embodying the purest morality we have attained, to be followed even at the cost of one's life. This is not the kind of strength required by the life and death struggle for survival, which is certainly better served by ruthlessness; vitality is more essential to it than morality. Most moral commandments would need an extremely difficult reinterpretation to make them agree with Darwinism in any of its forms; in fact, hardly anything suggesting moral qualities would be left. Nietzsche has shown that the 'new morality' thus required is the opposite of what we have called morality. There is no need, therefore, to discuss this theory further.*

Of much greater significance is the sociological theory. It claims that the good is not an absolute value, but what is good for society, and therefore developed by its influence.

---

* It is true that there have been attempts to make collaboration and mutual help the main principle in the life of plants and animals, but these attempts have failed to replace or even to influence Darwinism. Such phenomena exist, but seem to be of secondary importance. In any case, the biological explanation of morality is usually based on Darwinism.

There is certainly much truth in this theory; morality helps us to become social beings which we hardly are from birth. To see the effects of social influences will make it easier to distinguish the application of morality from morality itself. But there is something very surprising in the development of morality if we regard it from the social point of view.

Our main advances in the knowledge of the good are due to men who revolted against society and were attacked or executed by it. Moses was fiercely rejected by his people when he brought them the Ten Commandments; Socrates stood for a new conception of the good which we now recognize as the right one, but he was executed; Christ was crucified. How could these facts be understood if morality only stood for what society required?

Socrates was a philosopher; his fate, therefore, can be discussed most easily in philosophical terms. We find, surprisingly, that, from the social point of view, his executioners were right. To claim that there was a morality which was valid, not only for the citizens of Athens, but for every man, for slaves as well as for others, actually endangered the Greek city state. Such a claim was bound to undermine the cohesion of this particular society, and the lack of cohesion undoubtedly played its part in the destruction of the city states. Yet we can say today that morally Socrates was right, that he has contributed essentially to our knowledge of the good, and that, in this respect, his persecutors were wrong. This, however, goes towards proving the absoluteness of morality, for societies change, and a morality of the past, if it were only the product of a particular vanished society, could not be valid for us. Unless there is something absolute which remains the same for all ages and all men we could not say that Socrates was right; we could only judge him in the historical context, as an interesting historical figure. It is not society which develops a higher morality, pointing beyond itself; on the contrary, the higher morality is often developed in opposition to the existing society, by such men as Moses, Socrates, Christ or some of the later churchmen, heretics, reformers and philosophers who struggle against society, some of them even sacrificing their lives in order to create a more moral attitude. It is always the higher morality which gradually transforms society, and it can do so because, once something absolute is touched, it can be recognized as being right in all circumstances.

Again, difficult re-interpretations are needed to make the sociological theory agree with the facts. To give just one example of how far such interpretations can go: Durkheim, a psychologist of some importance, asserts that society has an unconscious idea of the good it will need in the next stage of its development. This idea becomes conscious first to single individuals, such as Socrates, but as society is still unconscious of it, this individual is treated as its enemy. However, he brings the idea into the open and thus makes society aware of its actual need, so that, after he had been persecuted or killed, society accepts the idea. Can we really believe in this personification of society? To reconcile the facts we know with society's unconscious awareness of its future seems far more difficult than to reconcile them with an absolute morality which this explanation is meant to replace.

Morality, after all, is fundamentally individual. There is no commandment addressed to society—that society should do this or that—the 'Thou' is essential. Yet if it is an appeal to the individual, the fact that single individuals experience this appeal first and stand up against society does not seem surprising. Certainly, education and punishment, whose part is emphasized by the sociological theory, are of great influence, but they are based on values; moral convictions must precede the decision of what is to be punished. The same applies to the administration of justice; it is meant to enforce what had been recognized as right; and though custom and prejudice gradually interfere and perhaps even dominate, it ought to be always redressed in the light of our moral knowledge. That morality is independent of society can also be seen once a society is guided solely by material considerations and social requirements; then morality is not developed, but has to be replaced by compulsion or incentives. We can appreciate to-day how important it would be if individuals stood up against society once again, so as to raise the moral level. They would certainly be treated as enemies of society. The commandments of the Sermon on the Mount, for instance, though we pay lip-service to them, are still far from acceptable in politics.

Another group of theories is based on psychology. There is no doubt that there is, in these theories too, a good deal of truth which can help to clear the ground. We are to a large extent the products of the processes which psychology describes. Much in human behaviour is determined by events which took place in the past and can no longer be changed; the discovery of the subconscious revealed a factor which is real and powerful. But psychology aims at the kind of certainty which we find in physics; its ideal is to show that we are entirely determined by experiences in the past upon which we had no influence, that we are at the mercy of factors which can explain—causally or statistically—our behaviour and which leave no room for free decisions. This conviction is used to represent morality as relative. Can it be accepted as the whole truth?

We have discussed the scope of psychology several times,★ so that we need not enter into this argument again. Psychology is concerned with how we think and feel, act and react, but

★ See pp. 3–4, 12–14, 24–6.

not with the fundamental concepts we apply; it explains how we use and misuse values, but not the values themselves; it traces the processes of judging, but not the standards upon which we base our judgments. Therefore, though it can show when we do not act freely, it is unable to say anything about our freedom as such.* There is clearly something more to morality than can be discovered by the methods of psychology.

It is mainly psychology which would make us use the terms 'good' and 'evil' in the same way as 'beautiful' and 'ugly'— that is, as onlookers, in the quasi-aesthetic way which we have mentioned. The experience of feeling responsible for our actions, however, proves conclusively that this attitude is insufficient in the moral sphere.

Further, there is the frequent assertion that morality is simply a matter of customs and therefore ever changing, dependent on age, nation, geography, and even on climate. This is true of the application of morality and its formulation; but does it apply to morality as such? I must confess that I have never been quite able to understand this claim. The chief moral commandments have in reality changed hardly at all and less than everything else. If we consider, for instance, the historical context of the Ten Commandments or of the Sermon on the Mount, we see that the states and nations with which the Jews came into contact at both these moments in history have completely disappeared; the very countries have been transformed, fertile plains have become deserts and forests rocky wildernesses; the climate has changed; practically the only things which have survived are these few sentences stating moral commandments.† They alone are in

---

* See pp. 5–6.

† Something similar applies to the embodiments of the other absolute values— poetry, sculpture, painting, architecture, age-old books of wisdom—but as we are not concerned with these here, we can leave them out of account. For a fuller treatment see P. Roubiczek, *Thinking towards Religion*, chs. 2 and 6.

their essence still valid—that is, still alive and of real influence in our lives. In contrast, the methods and views of science which we tend to regard as much more reliable have undergone many changes since then, and each change has invalidated previous theories.

Morality is as stable as we could possibly imagine anything to be which is part of human history. As man develops in an historical way, we find that morality, at first, also develops in accordance with different historical conditions; in early times, in primitive society, it hardly exists in the form in which we have been discussing it. Yet the surprising fact is, not that it develops at first in the same way as everything else, but that it suddenly becomes stable whenever and wherever a certain stage of development is reached. This happens in Judaism with the Ten Commandments and the later prophets, in Greece with the philosophers from Socrates onwards; it happens in Christianity, Buddhism, Confucianism, Taoism. From then onwards the moral achievements remain static, while almost everything else continues to change. Does this not indicate that something real is disclosed, which belongs essentially to man's nature, which differs from mere customs? The more so as the moral demands of the great religions are so very similar, even though at the time of their origin the different countries could not influence each other. The stability of morality is indeed striking, despite the changes in its interpretation and application.

The equation of morality with customs would also mean that moral questions can be decided by a majority vote. If morality were only what was customary with a nation, its majority could reliably decide which behaviour was moral and which not. It was David Hume who claimed that actions were right when they aroused in a majority of mankind a sentiment of moral approval. However, W. Lillie is more convincing when he says, refuting Hume: 'There are certainly cases where an individual judges an action to be right, although he knows that the majority of mankind and the majority of every group concerned with it dislike and feel moral disapproval of the action. One of the most characteristic manifestations of individual conscience is to make moral judgments different from those of the majority of the group to which the individual belongs.'[1] And we have seen that the individual can, like Socrates, be right, even against an overwhelming majority. Minority and majority do not count. What counts is the inner certainty, because the absolute is the same for all men and ages. When, therefore, someone touches upon the absolute, his knowledge of it will be gradually recognized and established. Thus moral questions cannot be settled by numbers.

Another group of theories tries to establish ethical relativity directly, in a purely philosophical way. This assertion can be made in many different forms, but at bottom it always tends to show that one moral code is as little justified as any other, that it is only a matter of taste if we prefer one and reject the other. A tribal code which permits cannibalism would be as well founded—or as unfounded—as Roman Stoicism or Christian morality. Bertrand Russell says that it is impossible to reject Nietzsche's teaching on philosophical grounds because it is 'internally self-consistent'; he only feels entitled to say that he dislikes it.[2] We can certainly sympathize with this statement; but is it correct? Is it really philosophically impossible to show conclusively that the values of the 'blond beast' are worse than Christian love?

These theories were mainly developed within Logical Positivism and, with the decline of that school, now have much less weight than once appeared. But several points are worth discussing because they show what is always implied in any theory which tries to make morality relative. It is true that, if morality depended on external conditions alone, the worst tribal code would really be as justified as any other.

The main objection to such statements is obvious—they underrate human intelligence. If they were merely a matter of taste, they could not be meaningfully discussed; but they are discussed and obviously can be and ought to be discussed. The Logical Positivists said that all value-judgments were akin to the statement 'I like sugar in my tea' which has to be believed without further discussion. But this is only a particular kind of value-judgment; moral ones are entirely different. If the all-important question 'What ought I to do?' could not be considered, then philosophy would have to abdicate. Several of the reasons why such an abdication is unnecessary are of general importance.

First, likes and dislikes—often mentioned in this context— need not be identical with value-judgments. We may dislike punishing a child and yet approve of it—a distinction which can increase our awareness as much as that between 'good' and 'right' which we have mentioned. In fact, moral demands are usually far too exacting to be liked; it is for that reason that they are rarely obeyed. Nevertheless, it is equally wrong to believe, as Kant did, that doing one's duty is only laudable if it is done with difficulty and against one's inclinations; occasionally it may be both laudable and agreeable. We must learn to distinguish different kinds of feelings from one another; likes and dislikes must be clearly separated from moral impulses. Such distinctions are often difficult, but they are possible. In actual experience, feeling responsible for a person, for instance, can be distinguished from feeling attracted by a person. The compelling quality of passion is different from the compelling quality of conscience. Instead of reducing the distinctness of morality by looking for apparent similarities—whether sociological, psychological, or purely logical—we should concentrate on its particular characteristics. As we are concerned here with feelings (we speak correctly of the feeling of responsibility, and recognize that the reactions of conscience are felt) it is essential to increase our sensitivity with the help of such distinctions.

The second objection rests on the fact that these characteristic differences between statements of preference and statements about morality can be discovered and discussed. It is true that a preference for certain colours, for instance, is merely a matter of taste; if one person prefers a red tie or dress and another a blue one, no further discussion is possible as long as harmony with other colours is not disturbed. But we cannot say that telling a lie is always better than speaking the truth; it may be so on certain very special occasions, but it cannot be made into a moral principle. Nor is it merely a matter of taste, of a purely subjective deliberation, to call a murder immoral. Certain value-judgments are based on taste or on individual preferences, but moral judgments are not, because they cannot be inverted, nor can two opposite views both be true. Therefore we can increase our knowledge by discussion.

Thus a complete scepticism—which is also advocated in this context—is really untenable. Such a scepticism would mean that anyone's moral view is completely private, because the concepts 'right' and 'good' cannot be defined; when using them, everyone means something different, and no decision about the correct meaning is possible. This is obviously false in the light of all that we have said; we need only think of murder, or of stealing, or of the stability of the moral commandments. But scepticism is tempting; it may allow us to shun responsibility. However, nobody ever acts on this basis if he is admitting moral considerations at all; if he thus has arrived at his conclusions after a careful scrutiny of all the factors involved, he will be convinced that his conclusions are of general validity.

The third objection is that moral commandments are not— as some Logical Positivists claim—mere imperatives. According to this view, to say 'This action is good' would simply mean 'Do this action'. It is true that the commandments are always expressed in the form of an imperative—'Thou shalt'— yet they are compelling because they correspond to a factor in man's nature which they make clear by their appeal. Logically it seems correct to say that imperatives, using 'shalt' or 'ought' and thus referring to future possibilities, have nothing in common with statements about present facts, expressed by the verb 'to be', and that therefore morality is not a fact. But this purely logical distinction is misleading; if it were not, the commandments could be easily dismissed as arbitrary. But since they are compelling, they must be rooted in facts which they thus also express. After all, the commandments do not deal exclusively with the future; they also enable us to judge past actions.

The Existentialist theories about morality will be discussed later. Some of them deny absolute morality and try to establish instead that every man creates his own; in their view morality is not determined by elements in man's nature, but is entirely arbitrary. Nevertheless, these Existentialists want to preserve responsibility, to show that man is responsible for what he is and what he does. In this they fail. Man, according to them, is responsible for his actions to himself, but as there is no given morality, he can constantly change the principles on which he bases his actions. Though most Existentialists deny it, this leads once more towards a concept of the absolute, for, to make sense, responsibility demands dependence on a trans- cendental which is absolute. To make sense, responsibility has to be, not only 'responsibility for' but also 'responsibility to ', and man himself is insufficient to give meaning to the latter, unless he at least admits the presence of transcendental elements in his own nature. Morality cannot be arbitrarily created; it must have authority.

For everyday life, however, the most important theory of the relativity of morals is probably that based on materialism —so much so that many people would hardly think of it as a theory, but consider it as realistic practice. Yet it discloses further gaps in the explanations which make morality relative.

The materialists want to achieve the greatest happiness for the greatest numbers. This sounds convincing and was originally meant to be humane, but it really avoids the main question; the happiness which is desired is not defined. We may try, as materialists, to keep our feet firmly on the ground and want everything to be of advantage to us; but what is to our real advantage? To be selfish and show it unashamedly, or to pretend at least to follow some moral code and to love our neighbour, or to love him genuinely and to obey our conscience? Embarrased by such questions, we may fall back on the statement that we simply want to be happy. But what kind of happiness do we want? To be able to follow every whim, to have enough money to fulfil every wish which happens to occur to us? But if we do this, we shall discover that some of our wishes lead us into actions which give us no pleasure and some of our actions come to appear vile to us; we need some further standards. Moreover, we want friends, and a happy family life. This needs at least mutual trust, and trust between people is hardly possible without the conviction that others try to act according to the same standards as we do ourselves. In other words: the need for the absolute value of the good will gradually make itself felt. Even mere usefulness easily leads to the question 'What is really worth doing?'—that is, what is really good—when the choice is not one of means for a particular end, but between different ends, as, for instance, between different kinds of careers. The prospect of earning more money will hardly, by itself, guarantee satisfaction with one's job.

Of course, the materialist sticks to the emphasis on material possessions. But, to gain these, he has to suppress the original impetus of materialist philosophy—which was concern for the equality of men, love of the underprivileged and the wish to establish justice for everybody. Dictatorship in the East and pressure of conformism in the West see to it that material achievements are valued most highly: of the many ways to happiness only this one is admitted, and the materialists do whatever is in their power to enforce it. Technical progress, increase in production and, in their wake, increase in wealth gradually degrade man, who should not live by bread alone. One cannot have it both ways: either goodness transcends material aims, or man's dignity is destroyed.

Finally, there are idealistic theories about morality. These go some way towards recognizing its absoluteness, but as they do not go the whole way, even these theories remain inconclusive.

The idealist usually accepts the traditional three absolute values—truth, goodness, beauty—as ultimate facts, without inquiring where they spring from. This is one of the attempts to establish humanism while rejecting religion. To prove their point, idealists tend to ask the question: 'Does not a humanist frequently behave more decently than a Christian? —and the answer is bound to be: 'Of course.' But does this really prove more than the strength of some and the weakness of other men? A more relevant question would be whether, as Christians claim, humanism is really the fruit of Christianity and will not survive if Christianity disappears. It did not survive in Nazi Germany nor in Communist Russia, and it is evidently endangered in our own society. However, as we do not know the future, history cannot provide us with unambiguous arguments.

Nevertheless, if we consult our experience, we see why we are not justified in stopping at the absolute values. Good actions of significance, under difficult circumstances, demand more than 'mere morality'—that is, more than a morality based on abstract concepts. They demand enthusiasm, complete surrender, the willingness to make sacrifices, perhaps even to sacrifice one's life, and they create a very particular kind of joy, a profound happiness. All these feelings cannot be kindled by obedience to the moral law alone, nor by the absolute values as such, but must spring from some deeper source which points beyond the moral law. Morality should spring from love, and Kierkegaard has shown convincingly, as we have seen, that the commandment to love one's neighbour, whatever one's feelings, presupposes an experience of the transcendental.* This is confirmed by another fact which we have already mentioned—that morality is in peril whenever moral laws are obeyed for the sake of lawfulness alone.† The Pharisees are the obvious example; their piety made them formulate more and more laws intended to prevent immoral actions, these laws then hardened into rules which became an end in themselves, and a dogmatic application of morality buried the source of love. Jesus had to attack them more fiercely than the obvious sinners, because this kind of obedience made them proud and ruthless. It can, of course, also lead to what Berdyaev has called 'the intolerable dullness of virtue.'

To make the absolute values self-sufficient, idealists, too — either consciously or unconsciously — make morality relative; their beliefs depend on the belief that man is

* See pp. 67–8.   † See p. 64.

fundamentally good and that evil is of minor importance. In fact, however, man has good and evil potentialities, and it is difficult to decide which are stronger; morality should lead to the recognition of both, so as to help us to find a firm basis for the good. Idealism, by minimizing the reality of evil, is likely to lead to disappointment, for the idealist, when confronted by the real power of evil, has to admit that belief in man's essential goodness is untenable; but faith in morality will then be weakened by the destruction of a belief upon which morality does not depend.

These are a few examples of how the theories which see morality as relative leave room for different conclusions. The survey has had to be brief, but I hope that what I have said has been sufficient to allow us now to sum up why all these explanations fail to do justice to morality.

When man, observing himself, discovers the presence of a moral order within his very being, he also becomes aware, whether he likes it or not, of a connexion with an objective order. In experience, morality is neither arbitrary nor dependent on other factors; though it is experienced subjectively, it forces us to recognize an objective relationship, a compelling order. The fact that morality raises so many problems arises precisely because it is absolute; otherwise there would be no need to pay so much attention to it. Why do we constantly feel the need to satisfy our consciences, why is it so tenacious that it makes itself felt even when we try to belittle and to dismiss it? Having no external power, it could be easily disregarded if it were dependent on man or men alone. As it implies an objective order, however, moral questions, as distinct from likes, dislikes and customs, can be meaningfully discussed. We feel that moral contradictions should be resolved, even though the application of the moral law to different situations is full of contradictions and leads to various decisions—a difficulty to which we shall return in a moment.

Being the expression of an objective order, the moral 'ought' is experienced as unconditional. It cannot be formulated conditionally as can such other demands as: 'If you want to play the violin well, you must practise every day.' There is no 'if'; all the attempts to introduce such a tempting condition—which usually took the form of promising rewards, or penalties, either in this life or the next—have harmed morality because they have paved the way for relativity. Even the question 'Why should I be moral?' is already immoral, because it is a request for a claim higher than morality.

The authority from which moral commandments issue is underived and unconditional, too. If it is fully experienced, it can override all planned and willed ends; it can work against one's self-interest, against the demands of the family or the political authority to which we apparently have to submit. H. H. Farmer has called the moral demand an 'inescapable claim'.[1] It is, not an order, but a claim, for we can reject it and try to suppress the voice of conscience; we may even reduce its force considerably if we ignore our consciences long enough. Yet the claim is inescapable: once it is fully understood, we cannot escape it however hard we try to disregard or reject it; we know that we ought to obey. This is experienced without any reference to any further authority; the authority of the claim is underived. It is based—as we have seen when discussing the 'Thou'*—on our personal experience of the demand itself.

At the same time, the absoluteness of the demand is vouched for by the fact that any situation in which we find ourselves, if it is seen in the light of morality, is completely changed; it acquires a new depth and significance. We feel

* See pp. 65-7.

that we are not simply faced with practical considerations and that opportunism will not do; our feeling of responsibility is at its strongest. This is so because a situation experienced as moral becomes an experience of freedom. The moral demand, because it is unconditional, implies that I am actually able to do what I ought to do, and it is only because I really experience this ability that I can no longer minimize my responsibility. If the moral demand were not unconditional it would have to be connected with 'ifs' and reservations. It is true that external and internal compulsions are often strong enough to prevent me from doing what I ought to do. Nevertheless, the absolute demand is justified; though I can be prevented from doing anything, by being imprisoned or physically incapacitated for instance, nobody can force me to do what I do not want to do if I am prepared to take the final risk—to sacrifice my life. Compulsion lost its power over Socrates, because he would rather die than submit.

One could perhaps raise objections to this confidence today which were unthinkable a short time ago—namely that there are new drugs, operations and psychological conditioning techniques which can change man's character and force him to do what he does not want to do. Thus any chance of asserting one's freedom in face of external compulsion seems to have gone. Yet in fact this new possibility gives more force to the argument that a situation, seen in the light of morality, acquires greater depth by becoming an experience of freedom. There are two reasons for this; first, if we look at these new capabilities merely from a practical point of view, their implications will not be fully appreciated and they will be misused, as some of them were in Nazi Germany; to understand this new situation, we have to recognize that it represents a grave moral problem, an increased responsibility. We shall have no choice but to introduce absolute morality into our considerations, for a relative morality will always allow us to defend some cases of the use of such practices, which will inevitably lead to a blurring of the boundaries of what might be defensible as a lesser evil and what not. Second, if we consider that we could be prevented from choosing death as a way of saving our freedom, we are still confronted by death—by a change of personality so complete that we do not survive as the person we are. Moreover, any observer would feel most poignantly that everything which deserves the name 'human' is in danger of being destroyed.

The failure of all theories which represent morality as relative shows, too, why a religious view can best do justice to morality. The word 'religion', however, has to be understood in this context as it is in Kierkegaard's Existentialism—not as a system of dogmatic statements and moral rules, but as a realistic description of the reality we experience.

Morality requires a certain metaphysical outlook: man must be free, his individual deeds must matter. No scientific theory can ever find a place for man's freedom, nor can it show that his deeds, however insignificant externally, are of consequence—that is, touch upon his 'absolute relationship to the absolute'. From any point of view, after all, it is difficult to realize that minute actions of minute individuals are of more than slight significance. Nor, as we have seen, is morality in isolation able to reach so far unless it includes the conception of sin.* Even if it is experienced only in a dim form, morality points beyond itself.

Morality also requires an impulse from something beyond human nature. Absolute values must have a basis, they must spring from somewhere, and this 'somewhere' must be more than nature plus man for it is not sufficient to explain them; they manifest an influence from the transcendental. This is

* See pp. 62–3.

confirmed by the nature of responsibility, which we have discussed; it cannot be simply a 'responsibility for', but must also be a 'responsibility to', and it acquires real significance only if it is a responsibility to something higher than man.* It leads us, therefore, beyond the earthly world. Morals do not belong entirely to this world.

Religion, by taking these aspects of morality into account, gives objectivity to moral values. Because these values are personal and demand personal participation if they are to become real, we always tend to fear that they are 'merely subjective'—doubtful, that is, or unjustified. This gives an additional reason for finding religion desirable, though, as we have said, this is not a sufficient reason to accept it. Yet as these aspects of morality are aspects of our actual experience, desirability is transcended by another criterion—the objective order which religion expresses is found at work in morality.† Religion and morality are interdependent.

Their interdependence is firmly rooted in the personal quality of morality. We experience morality as a feeling of personal loyalty rather than as the demands of an impersonal law; the moral commandment, because it addresses me, is a personal obligation and one which is probably most strongly felt when it is not obeyed. We have several times had to stress that to follow rules for their own sake is insufficient. We need not only do what is right, but we must also do it for the right motives; in the words of T.S. Eliot:

> The last temptation is the greatest treason:
> To do the right deed for the wrong reason.[1]

The motive, however, can only be recognized by ourselves; to others we can always pretend (we can also pretend to ourselves, but then we are completely cut off from morality).

* See pp. 88–9.　　　† See p. 92.

We must be ready to risk destroying a false impression even against our own interests. This exacting honesty can only be understood because we, as individual persons, face that reality which becomes objective in religion.

It is true that we cannot avoid moral contradictions and the conflicts arising from them. The moral law has to be applied under different circumstances and its application is not necessarily clear for all occasions. It cannot be extended to take account of every circumstance, for then it would exclude our personal participation. Some area of uncertainty must be left to allow for individual decisions; a moral decision must be our own, so as to make sure that we do the right deed for the right reason. Thus we can experience conflicting loyalties or duties, a conflict, for example, between our obligations to our family, which demand a certain amount of selfishness, and those to our neighbour, which demand great unselfishness; or the conflict between the compelling duty to defend our country and the absolute commandment 'Thou shalt not kill.' But whenever we experience a serious conflict of that kind—whenever, for instance, we face honestly the possible justifications of patriotism and pacifism—we also experience the existence of that reality with which religion claims to deal. Why, otherwise, should we feel so intensely in such conflicts rather than simply giving in or choosing the easiest way out? The pressures behind opportunism seem stronger than we are, and yet we struggle desperately to come to the right decision, even if, in the end, our decision is that of the majority. Conflicts within morality cannot be avoided and we might expect that this fact is sufficient to invalidate both morality and religion; instead, however, it is their strength which is revealed by such conflicts.

This close relationship between morality and religion can also be appreciated from a different point of view. On the one hand, the danger of ethics, of mere morality, is the following of rules for the sake of following rules. If this is done, the purely negative commandments—for instance 'Thou shalt not kill'—become more prominent than the positive ones, such as 'Thou shalt love', for we can state unequivocally the actions which are always against the law, while the positive commandments cannot be stated in such a definitive way because they must leave room for personal decisions. Such morality, however, becomes a dead collection of prohibitions. If it is to come to life, morality needs the fullness of the transcendental world from which it originates. On the other hand, the danger of religion is that it turns into metaphysical contemplation, with strong human fancies or abstract theological speculation playing a large part, and thus loses its connexion with man's life. Morality and religion, to remain pure and alive, depend on each other. Their true relationship has been most beautifully stated by John Oman, when he says: 'If religion, without morality, lacks a solid earth to walk on, morality, without religion, lacks a wide heaven to breathe in.'[1] Without morality, religion is always in danger of being estranged from life, falling prey to unwarranted assertions; without religion, morality is always in danger of degenerating into rigidity or even cruelty. Their true relationship has been distorted again and again, but it is so strong that it has also, again and again, been restored.

We have said that, when discussing morality, we cannot rely on material or scientific proofs; yet if we admit experience as evidence, as we must do because experience alone makes morality accessible, it is belief in an absolute morality which agrees with the facts.

CHAPTER VI

KIERKEGAARD AND EXISTENTIALISM

Existentialist philosophers try to grasp man as he actually is, as he experiences himself in his specific, historical situation. Moreover, some of those Existentialists who do not go to extremes—in my view the best ones—and some philosophers influenced by Existentialism deal also with human relationships and see man among men, not in isolation. These attempts are perhaps the most hopeful signs in the recent development of philosophy. It is true that, in the older metaphysical systems, the individual was in the centre, too, but only as an abstract entity; it was a general idea of him, *the* human mind, which was thought of as confronting the universe. Instead, we now find the central place given to ourselves and the problems which harrass us in our lives.

This shift of emphasis, as we have said, requires the application of the 'subjective method'. The difficulty which thus arises is indicated by the ambiguity of the word 'subjective'. While the word 'objective' can be used without further explanation, the word 'subjective' is often taken to mean 'biased, falsified by prejudice' or even as a synonym for wishful thinking. But, especially when we talk about the 'subjective method', it ought to mean nothing more nor less than a particular approach, of equal validity to the objective method, to be used where objectivity is insufficient—that is where personal participation is required for the gaining of any knowledge at all. We have seen that this is the case when we try to deal with personal experiences, morality, values, faith. This implies, therefore, that the subjective method should be, in its own way, just as reliable as the objective—say, the scientific—method actually is. But does not the combination of 'subjective' and 'reliable method' appear a contradiction in terms?

To achieve reliability in this way is difficult because, once we accept evidence drawn from our experience, bias and prejudice can easily creep in, and it is hard to make the right discriminations because this method has been neglected for centuries. Pascal, the early predecessor of Existentialism, already felt, three hundred years ago, that he could not achieve this kind of clarity without a conscious effort. As soon as he says: 'The heart has its reasons which reason does not know', he also recognizes that 'men often take their imagination for their heart'. He is constantly afraid that the 'heart' may be replaced by 'fancies', because 'the heart is wanting'. But he never doubts that 'we know truth, not only by the reason, but also by the heart, and it is in this last way that we know first principles; and reason, which has no part in it, tries in vain to impugn them.'[1] He died before he could finish his main work and was thus unable to work out an appropriate method. This was left to Kierkegaard who not only shows—as we have seen in the fourth chapter—how fruitfully the method can be used, but also reveals some of its main characteristics and thus helps us to apply it correctly.

His starting point is the distinction between knowledge and faith—knowledge meaning in this context (and always in this chapter) knowledge achieved by a conscious effort of thinking. His position is that everything which we can know is impossible to believe. This may sound like an exaggeration; but we can see what he means. Because we cannot acquire all the knowledge we need by our own efforts, we must, in practice, often believe others; yet in principle we could ourselves test all knowledge based on the objective method. We could, for

Kierkegaard and Existentialism

instance, learn to make scientific experiments ourselves, so as to decide whether the conclusions based on them are acceptable, or we could look up the documents so as to see whether such statements as 'Kierkegaard was born in 1813' correspond to the facts. Belief is only of secondary, practical importance. Yet with faith, belief is of the essence, because it refers to the divine sphere which transcends man immensely and therefore cannot be fully known. Here we have to perform the act of faith; we need a constantly renewed willingness to accept what is beyond proof, we must risk the 'jump into the abyss' which can be justified, not by a preceding knowledge of its result, but only by the ensuing experience.* Thus faith is not, as is often assumed, a weak substitute for knowledge, to be replaced by it as soon as possible; the two are fundamentally different.

We must acknowledge two different kinds of truth. Their difference becomes obvious as soon as we think of an encyclopaedia. Such a work contains a very large number of correct statements which are based on knowledge; but we shall hardly consult it to discover that kind of truth by which we live. The subjective method should reveal a truth which, in contrast to factual information, can become a personal experience and thereby have a deep influence upon what we believe and do—an influence such as is exercised by any kind of faith.

To discover the truth by which we live, we must start from personal experience and base our ideas on it, not *vice versa*. This is the central condition for all Existentialists, who never omit to emphasize that 'the personal is the real'. Kierkegaard insists: 'The attempt to infer existence from thought is a contradiction. For thought takes existence away from the real and thinks it by abrogating its actuality, by

* See pp. 56–61.

translating it into the sphere of the impossible.'[1] He illustrates this statement by discussing the equilateral triangle which never occurs in perfect geometrical regularity in nature; such a regularity is achieved only when all actual natural conditions are disregarded. We could also extend this to the derivation of abstract concepts, for these form the basis of the thought to which Kierkegaard refers. For instance, if we arrive at such a concept as 'table', all particular characteristics of real tables—colour, weight, shape and so on—are eliminated to enable us to apply the concept to any table whatever. We have created the concept 'by abrogating actuality' and translated it 'into the sphere of the impossible', for *the* table without special characteristics does not exist. Therefore it would be wrong to start from the abstract concept in order to 'infer existence'. Yet this, as Kant had shown already, is exactly what has been done in abstract metaphysical systems, and the attack has to be renewed because, despite Kant, Hegel uses the abstract concept 'spirit', Schopenhauer 'the Will', the materialists 'matter' as the basis of their systems. Kierkegaard's Existentialist attack is much more direct than that of Kant—and it convinces directly. We must start from our personal experience of existence.

Such a start requires us to apply, constantly and correctly, the subjective method. Kierkegaard is aware of its difficulties: 'It is commonly assumed that no art or skill is required in order to be subjective. To be sure, every human being is a bit of a subject, in a sense. But now to strive to become what one already is: who would take the pains to waste his time on such a task, involving the greatest imaginable degree of resignation? . . . But for this very reason alone it is a very difficult task, the most difficult of all tasks in fact.'[2]

To make us aware of the magnitude of this task, he shows again and again how much courage is required when one abandons the security of noncommittal abstract speculation for the risk of self-commitment, and thus he prepares his readers for a full understanding of his examples. One has to face the 'fear and trembling' of Job or Abraham which we have discussed; in the hope of finding absolute certainty one has to be prepared to endure a state of mind where all certainty has gone.

What the method itself means is perhaps best illuminated when Kierkegaard says 'An objective acceptance of Christianity is either paganism or thoughtlessness.'[1] Christianity is a way of life; to accept it as an interesting line of thought, as an abstract explanation of the universe, or as ritual, but without acting upon it, makes it well nigh meaningless. The subjective method always establishes first the relationship between creed, life and action; to give reality to the creed, the method involves us in its consequences. We must be willing to commit ourselves to what we believe so as to understand its meaning through the actual experience which it gives us.

Actions will only produce the right kind of subjective insight, however, if they are based on the right attitude. Kierkegaard demands this attitude when he observes: 'The majority of men are subjective towards themselves, while being objective against all others, terribly objective sometimes— but the real task is exactly the opposite; to be objective towards oneself and subjective towards all the others.'[2] We should not give in to our natural tendency to be severe towards others and lenient to ourselves, for we shall understand others only if we try to understand them from within, by attempting to make their experiences our own. When confronting ourselves, however, we need a certain detachment to enable us to distinguish bias and prejudice from that self which is common to all men, but becomes accessible through personal experience alone. In other words: we always need the contrast between objectivity and subjectivity; therefore we have to be alive to it both outside us, where objectivity seems more natural, and also inside us, where biased subjectivity tends to blind us. We need actions because they create a relationship between outside and inside, and they will increase our understanding if both our objective and subjective attitudes are right. God alone, according to Kierkegaard, is 'the absolute subjectivity'; for Him outside and inside are one, and what appears objective and thus foreign to us, is known to him fully from within. We have to make objectivity serve the subjective method.

In this way we can achieve what Kierkegaard regards as 'the maximum of attainment'—namely 'simultaneously to sustain an absolute relationship to the absolute end, and a relative relationship to relative ends'.[1] This may sound obvious once it is said; of course, we should take the absolute much more seriously than anything relative; but it is extremely difficult to achieve. For instance, we are all prone to be more concerned about the loss of a large sum of money or a trespassing against the social code if it embarrasses us on an occasion which may be important for our career than about a grave sin which remains unknown to others or which is condoned by society. We forgive ourselves laziness of the heart more easily than a mistake which has damaging practical consequences. But once we are really able to look at relative ends with that detachment which Kierkegaard described so well when discussing social distinctions—as a cloak which has to be cast off*—and are, at the same time, deeply committed to the absolute, our philosophy will begin to develop in the right direction.

The difference between the usual philosophical approach

* See p. 71.

and that of the Existentialists could be summed up in the following way. Most of the non-Existentialist philosophers start from things, then include the person, but only as an abstract entity, as an abstract thinker, and return to the things again, so as to gain objective knowledge. Kierkegaard starts from the person, then includes the things, in order to gain and clarify personal experience, and returns to the person again, so as to achieve the right kind of subjectivity. He wants to turn our attention to inner experiences; his aim is inwardness.

There is, however, another contrast between the two methods: the reliability which each can achieve is different, because it is based on two different kinds of certainty.

The results of the objective method can be tested, proved, and once they are proven, satisfactorily communicated to others, because they can be accepted without further inquiry. Yet they are never final. Although the facts do not change, their interpretation, as the development of science shows, does, and the discovery of new facts incessantly leads to alterations or to the complete replacement of scientific theories. Reliability is great, thus making the technical application of science possible; but it must never be taken for absolute certainty, for this would hinder further developments.

The subjective method remains dependent on constantly renewed experiences; its results cannot be accepted once and for all, because they always have to be translated into our own experience. As personal participation is required, an area of uncertainty must be left open, as we have seen, so as to allow for personal decisions.* Thus the application of this method is constantly beset by difficulties and dangers; none of its results can be taken for granted. Yet once certainty is achieved, it is absolute. When we fully experience goodness, for instance, we can no longer doubt that we have touched

* See pp. 77–8, 97.

upon a reality which we must accept unconditionally, if we are to do justice to our experience. Therefore the results of the subjective method have the stability of the Ten Command-ments or the Sermon on the Mount*—a stability unequalled in the sphere of the objective method. These results are final, yet they cannot be fully communicated; they must again and again be made our own experience if they are to become our own conviction and part of our lives. Thus there is always a risk; nothing prevents us from making the wrong decision. But the risk is worth taking, for, while science can completely reshape the external form of our life, the possible positive results of the subjective method alone have a profound significance for our inner, personal development.

With Kierkegaard, too, difficulties and dangers do not disappear. We have mentioned possible criticisms before.† In his view Christianity is most absurd, because no rationalist could ever believe that God became the lowliest of men and was executed, but he holds that this makes Christianity the best religion, because it thus requires the strongest possible act of faith. Yet Christianity, though transcending reason, can surely be served by it as well. Kierkegaard sees man and God in utter contrast, separated completely by the gulf of the absurd; yet there must be at least a spark of the divine in man to make him want to risk 'the jump into the abyss'. His emphasis on the irrational paradox also excludes reason too completely, and his constant demand for despair, despite all its positive aspects, pays too little attention to the gospels as good news, to the significance of joy.

The most disturbing weakness, perhaps, is that his demand that we should include our own historical situation in our con-siderations makes him too dependent on his own time. He says: 'Passion is the culmination of existence for an existing indi-

---

* See pp. 83–4.   † See pp. 9–10 and 61–2.

vidual',[1] and he attacked the age in which he lived as wretched because it was without passion. His identification of passion and inwardness is hardly acceptable to-day. The nationalistic and ideological movements of our time have shown that passion can be more destructive than the lukewarmness which Kierkegaard attacks; clearer distinctions are necessary. It is true that he recognizes the indifference of his age so clearly that many of his strictures still apply, as when he says: 'Our age is not willing to stop with faith, with its miracle of turning water into wine, it goes further, it turns wine into water.'[2] But the dangerous overemphasis on passion becomes obvious again and again—when he claims, for example, that, if a pagan believes in his idols passionately, while a Christian has a lukewarm belief, it is the pagan and not the Christian who believes as one should believe. We certainly need both, the right kind of feeling and the right belief. Kierkegaard warns us himself that the truth of a proposition is not a thing that can be asserted once for all, but that it is relative to the intention of the asserter and depends ultimately upon what the proposition is asserted *against*. This may not be generally true, but we have to bear it in mind in connexion with some aspects of his teaching.

However, as the subjective method must leave room for personal decisions, what matters most is that it should ensure that we move in the right direction. If this is the case, any error will lead to a further clarification; only if we move in a totally wrong direction will a philosophy be seriously misleading. Kierkegaard never loses the sense of the direction in which he ought to move. We can see this in his life, and if we consider it, we are less likely to be misled by the shortcomings of his ideas.

For Kierkegaard himself, the dangers were insignificant; having a firm foothold in Christianity, he was able to define his own position precisely. He saw himself, not as one of the prophets, nor as 'as an apostle who brings something from God, with authority', but as a martyr: 'My task is not to make room authoritatively, but to make room through suffering.'[1] He knew, too, that 'it is easier to become a Christian when I am not a Christian than to become a Christian when I am one';[2] rarely can the handicap of the diluted Christianity with which we are imbued from childhood onwards have been so succinctly described. But he recognized that 'in all eternity it is impossible for me to compel a person to accept an opinion, a conviction, a belief. But one thing I can do: I can compel them to take notice.'[3] It is to this task that he devoted his life, living his philosophy and showing both the humility and courage which it demanded.

His martyrdom is strikingly seen in one of his most painful struggles. He attacked the *Corsair*, a satirical journal published in his home town, Copenhagen, which ridiculed persons prominent in public life in such a malicious way that, though most responsible people hated it, none had dared to attack it. Kierkegaard did, fully aware of the consequences. He knew that his publications could not compete with the popularity of the journal and that he would be made the laughing stock of the whole town for many months; in fact for several years he was molested in the streets. But he achieved what he wanted—he forced people to take notice. The majority, it is true, only laughed at him, but a few understood and they preserved his works and memory. In short, he provoked ridicule—a truly modern martydom!* Only inner greatness

---

* This account of the struggle follows Kierkegaard's own. Mr. E. L. Bredsdorff, however, has recently pointed out that, at the beginning, Kierkegaard probably did not expect the martyrdom which, in retrospect, he appears to have been aiming for by his attack. But as Kierkegaard constantly relived his past in order to discover its true meaning (see p. 120), his later understanding of what he had done seems nevertheless both relevant and trustworthy.

and certainty have the strength to face it, and his diaries show that it was achieved at the cost of agonizing pain and suffering. He likened it to being trampled to death by geese.

In all his struggles he subordinated his person to his message. Towards the end of his life, after years of hesitation, he risked another attack—on the established Danish Lutheran Church, accusing its dignitaries of exercising power and living in great comfort, while preaching Christian virtues to others. Again at the cost of great suffering, he forced people to take notice, showing this time perhaps even more clearly what it means to be a Christian. He died at the age of 42—an old man before his time—after withdrawing from the bank the last of his money, exhausting at the same time his physical and his financial resources in the service of his beliefs. But he died in peace, in the knowledge that he had achieved what he could, and in the hope that the living would listen more readily to the words of one who was dead—a hope which has been abundantly fulfilled. He made one mistake, however. He believed that the individual is either lost in the dizziness of unending abstraction, or saved for ever in the reality of religion—overlooking that man could also be lost in the dizziness of Existentialism.

So far we have concentrated mainly on the positive aspects of Existentialism, and we shall return to them because it is the purpose of this book to show how this philosophy can help us to arrive at results which we can accept. But, to be able to appreciate the positive achievements correctly, we must also be aware of its weaknesses. The dangers which are of small importance for Kierkegaard assume different proportions in contemporary Existentialism, and we can see why. Kierkegaard uses the Existentialist approach as a method, to bring to life morality and Christianity; he creates a balance between existence (man's actual experience) and essence (man's nature

in its relationship to external reality and to the transcendental).*
Once Existentialism is pursued as an end in itself, however,
existence alone is admitted and essence is ignored—that is,
all the conditions and limitations inherent in man's nature are
neglected and experience can no longer be safely guided.
Thus all the latent dangers of Kierkegaard's teaching are
considerably increased and come to the fore.

We shall discuss this transformation of Existentialism and
some of its modern representatives in the next chapter. But,
so as not to lose contact with its positive elements, I intend
to discuss first how even some of the extreme manifestations
of Existentialist thought are connected with the more difficult
aspects of Kierkegaard's great achievements. The following
analysis refers, therefore, not to all Existentialists, but only
to what I shall call 'absolute Existentialism'—namely to the
doctrines of those Existentialists who believe that existence
can be grasped in isolation and that, by isolating it, we can
achieve absolute, ultimate knowledge.

Kierkegaard's central demand is that we should risk the
'jump into the abyss'; man is separated from God by an
enormous gulf; therefore he can achieve neither the good
nor faith by his own efforts; he must risk the leap into the
unknown.† Yet as the gulf is one between man and God, the
risk, if taken, can yield its own reward, for it can establish a
relationship to God. Once God is dismissed, however, as He
is by absolute Existentialism which must be atheist, the further
bank of the gulf, so to speak, disappears; the gulf simply
becomes emptiness, the complete void. Thus nothingness,
Le Néant, das Nichts, becomes the central experience, and as it
is central it is passionately embraced. Man, instead of risking
the leap into the unknown, plunges himself into nothingness,

---

* For the distinction between 'existence' and 'essence' see p. 11.
† For this and the following see pp. 56–61.

because he thus seems truly to face the core of his being.

This acceptance of nothingness becomes possible because the concept of the absurd also acquires a different significance. Kierkegaard emphasizes the absurd in order to bring about the strongest possible act of faith; to become fully aware of the absurdity of life or of Christianity is for him a way of experiencing them most meaningfully. Only by recognizing the absurdity of existence, so Kierkegaard believes, do we leave all superficial thought behind and discover within ourselves that reality which is the basis and justification of religion. But once the transcendental is dismissed altogether, the absurd itself becomes the final aim, for it seems to confirm that we are honest, that we are really facing reality without succumbing to illusions. It is a triumph to arrive at the absurd, and there is no further attempt to make it meaningful. Absurdity is identified with profundity.

The absolute paradox undergoes a similar transformation. For Kierkegaard it gives substance to hope; despite all the dread which apparent meaninglessness creates, there is still an unfathomable positive element in experience; this element cannot solve the paradox because it can only be felt and not expressed, but the paradox becomes the way to a positive experience. The absurd is conquered by its own paradoxical nature, for thanks to the paradox both dread and the absurd can lead to a harmony which transcends reason. But once the absurd is accepted and even enjoyed for itself alone, anything paradoxical is welcomed, for the paradoxes seem to confirm that we have been led to the most conclusive results of thought. The transcendental is thus replaced by the irrational. We shall discuss its different aspects in the last chapter, but we can see at once what the emphasis on the irrational implies. The concept itself means that which is beyond reason, but it can be interpreted in two main ways. It can be seen as a mystery which, when it is experienced, discloses a meaning transcending reason—and this is as it is interpreted by Kierkegaard—or as a completely meaningless destruction of reason, which is how the absolute Existentialists see it. These thinkers seek it everywhere and overemphasize it when they find it, so as to break down the influence of reason entirely.

As a result, we are confronted in their philosophy with an existential situation which is almost the opposite of Kierkegaard's. Nothingness, absurdity, the paradoxical nature of experience and the irrational must needs lead to despair, too. But while Kierkegaard forces us to face despair because he believes that its very depth will show that man has a reliable foothold in reality, the absolute Existentialists see meaningless despair, too, as an end in itself and as a desirable state of mind. There is no doubt that their despair is sincere, but it is not allowed to run its course; it is made the basis of philosophizing. Yet it is thus robbed of any further depth.

Despair as the final result of thought and experience means that fear and trembling, *Angst*, become the most basic quality of man's existence. This kind of dread is seen as a necessary achievement, for only by it is man able to appreciate fully the nature of existence. All those who do not live in this state of mind are supposed to be cut off from reality. Now it is certainly true for many men that fear is their most fundamental experience, and to emphasize it may be a challenge which is of special importance in our present situation. Complacency has hardly ever been as dangerous as it is today. But the emphasis on dread leads to one-sidedness; for the Christian or for anyone rooted in a faith trust and hope are more basic states of mind. Kierkegaard's despair leaves the way open for these other feelings; extreme Existentialism bars it, thus excluding important parts of man's nature. Instead, we often find—especially in Sartre and some of his followers—the choice of repulsive subjects which allow us to see nothing but the sordid, thus providing despair with what is obviously a superficial support. It is hard not to feel that despair can also be chosen as an easy way out; if everything is hopeless, we need not take any trouble; we can throw up our hands.

In general, though not entirely, Existentialism is saved from this danger, because despair is its source rather than its result. This philosophy developed mainly between the two wars, and since the Existentialists feel most acutely the catastrophes looming over mankind, they are also aware of man's questionable status and his frailty. It is true that the danger of relaxation is ever present—as when Heidegger succumbed to Nazism and Sartre became a Communist—but it is not final. Because Existentialism stems from despair, the apparent claims of the historical situation are transcended by the awareness of man's frailty—by the awareness of death.

There is no doubt that this constant reinforcement of despair and concentration on death can lead to morbidity and undermine our determination to fight for aims we recognize as desirable, or to give meaning to our lives. Nevertheless, the mystery of death—even more than that of birth—is bound to invalidate all the false convictions which survive from the Age of Reason and which we have discussed.* Purely rational thought, though it can explain the causes of death in scientific terms, can never account for the fact that we can die at any moment and are beings who, in any case, must die sooner or later. The length of our lives seems to be fixed in a purely arbitrary way which, being inexplicable, defeats the powers of reason. The rationalist has to disregard death or to deny its importance. Emphasis on death is common to Kierkegaard and the later Existentialists; for Kierkegaard, too, our being is an 'existence towards death', an illness which must needs

* See chapter 1.

lead to death. Again, however, there is an essential difference. For Kierkegaard, death is a challenge because the knowledge of its inevitability confronts us constantly with eternity and infinity, so that we are constantly forced to focus our attention upon the transcendental. For the extreme Existentialists, death supports all the negative experience upon which they concentrate; it is the final proof that life is meaningless.

The absolute Existentialists, as we have called them, are prevented from applying the subjective method correctly, because they exclude objectivity completely and replace reality entirely by feeling. What they consider to be the centre of existence—nothingness—is certainly a feeling which is experienced very strongly. We can feel emptiness, a complete void within ourselves, and it can lead to such despair that nothing but our destruction seems to make sense. Yet this feeling of nothingness must not be mistaken for a statement about external reality. In external reality we can only experience *something;* emptiness is only grasped as a space limited by objects and in contrast to them. If there is really nothing, we do not grasp anything. This sounds like a truism, but the mistake that we can grasp nothingness as an external fact is at the very basis of much Existentialist thought.

Negation has different functions in external reality and inner experience. In the material world, or in the historical account of man, negation (which helps to create the term 'nothingness') has a purely logical function; it never refers to non-existence, but always to something which exists. In order to understand, for instance, the statement 'Square circles do not exist', one has to know both squares and circles; if one asserts 'Absolute democracy does not exist', knowledge of the theory and practice of actual democracies is presupposed. In inner experience, however, negation refers to something real; there are positive and negative values, such as good and

evil, beauty and ugliness, both equally real; there is the contrast
between positive and negative feelings, such as joy and sorrow,
interest and indifference; we can experience a full life and
deadening emptiness; despair is just as real as satisfaction.
The negative can even be so real that it destroys all positive
certainty. The Existentialists frequently see their inner experience as belonging to the outside world and as its explanation; they project their despair into the world and see everything as part of it. As objectivity is rejected and anything
which could be objectively grasped is disregarded, the world,
man, the absolute lose all the characteristics which could
make them real; nothingness, as Nietzsche predicted and
Heidegger confirms, grows until it swallows everything.
Nothing is left—except nothingness.

Yet the connexion with the positive roots of Existentialism
is not entirely destroyed. The growth of a sense of nothingness is acutely felt, so acutely that it awakens a desperate
longing for some positive achievement. It is experienced as
a threat which has to be faced. Therefore both Sartre and
Heidegger demand an 'authentic life'—a way of life which
transcends all our blindness and easy make-believe and meets
this threat. Despair and the experience of growing nothingness should lead to a life which is really positive and worth
living, a life which cannot be shattered by the negative or
even terrifying experiences and insights which, if we are
honest, we cannot escape.

It is true that this way of life is not achieved and hardly
indicated by the absolute Existentialists themselves. Yet by
showing the ultimate consequences of their line of thought,
they confront the exaggerated rationalism of the Age of
Reason, which is still with us, with an exaggerated irrationalism,
and thus make us aware of both the extremes which we must
avoid. We are enabled to find our way between the Scylla

of absolute reason and the Charybdis of absolute unreason, and some of the less extreme Existentialists, following Kierkegaard more closely, begin to point out the way. In the next two chapters we shall first discuss absolute Existentialism in greater detail, and then turn to Martin Buber, so as to show another positive form of Existentialism.

CHAPTER VII

SOME ASPECTS OF FRENCH
AND GERMAN EXISTENTIALISM

Contemporary existentialist philosophy has developed in a great variety of ways. In France, Jean-Paul Sartre and his followers are atheists, Gabriel Marcel is a Roman Catholic, and Albert Camus's humanism is distinctly different from Sartre's. In Germany, Martin Heidegger and his school are atheists (at least for all practical purposes; they admit the possibility of a new religion in the future); but Heidegger has deeply influenced Christian thinkers, such as Romano Guardini; and Karl Jaspers is a theist and in a general way religious, though not a Christian. In England, it has been mainly such Christian thinkers as Herbert Farmer, Donald MacKinnon, John Macmurray who have taken notice of Existentialism. Martin Buber bases his philosophy on Jewish thought; Nikolas Berdyaev is a Christian, but of a most unorthodox kind. This brief enumeration, by no means exhaustive of course, is perhaps sufficient to indicate that Existentialism, though often chaotic, has opened up fertile new ground.

To give an idea of the wide range of Existentialism, I want once more to concentrate on what I have called 'absolute Existentialism'*—that is, mainly on Sartre and Heidegger and their schools, though I shall refer to some other thinkers as well, especially to Jaspers. All those who are Christian or religious accept at least some of Kierkegaard's thought unchanged. As we have already discussed his thought, a discussion of the other extreme will best help to indicate the

* See p. 110.

potentialities of this philosophy. It should become clear that there is a common basis to all Existentialism, for some of the elements mentioned before will reappear. If we are aware both of the common basis and of some of the most contradictory conclusions arising from it, we shall be able to understand the method of Existentialist thinking and thus understand also those ideas which cannot be included here. The negative extremes, moreover, will help us to appreciate the positive achievements better—the achievements which we have discussed before and to which we shall return in the next chapter.

Absolute Existentialism, according to our definition, is the attempt to make existence alone the basis of philosophy and of ultimate knowledge. It is founded on the belief that—as many Existentialists put it—'existence precedes essence'. This belief has several implications.

To begin with, this statement naturally draws attention to the birth of the individual, to the mystery of the origin of his existence, which we have mentioned* and which is easily overlooked by concentration on the essence common to all men of all ages. Most Existentialists echo the bewilderment of Pascal and Kierkegaard and give it greater force. Rationalism is made even more unacceptable, but at the cost of making it impossible to find answers to any of the problems with which philosophy usually claims to deal; irrationalism takes on the power of a principle and prepares the way for meaninglessness and despair. Thus Georges Bataille, a disciple of Sartre, states:

If I think of my coming into the world—bound up with birth, and beyond that, with the union of a man and a woman, and with the moment of that union—a unique chance decides the possibility of this self that I am; indeed the wild improbability of the mere being without which, for me, nothing would exist. The slightest change

* See pp. 57.

in the series of which I am the term, and instead of the self avid to be myself, there would only have been some other, and as for myself, there would have been only a nothingness, as complete as if I were dead.[1]

I have quoted at some length in order to show how the positive element in the idea—the making us aware of the mystery of birth and preventing any escape into superficiality —is gradually overlaid by paradoxical elements which are logical, but which hardly make sense. Obviously I can only discuss my existence and not my non-existence, for if I did not exist, I could not say 'I'. Such surreptitious shifts of emphasis are inevitable if existence is to be enhanced at the expense of anything else; lacking content, it seems inevitably to acquire some mystical quality. But as the transcendental, the only possible source of any true mysticism, is excluded, this mysticism must remain vague and uncertain. Mysticism should have a content which transcends understanding; the mere evocation of a similar kind of feeling with the help of paradoxes is insufficient.

The isolation of existence demands in general that too exclusive attention be paid to the single individual. We are connected with the world by what is covered by the term 'essence'—by common human nature, by general laws upon which we can rely. It is true that, at the same time, a full knowledge of our nature, based on inner experience, requires personal participation and that only thus does reality become entirely real to us; we have had to refer frequently to the claim that 'the personal is the real'. In absolute Existentialism, however, this claim is transformed into 'the personal is the *only* real' and the claim is made that I can know nothing but my own existence. Yet this is clearly wrong; if it were not, even inner experiences would become impossible. We become conscious of our own existence, of the 'I', by meeting others— by meeting the 'Thou', as we shall see in the next chapter;

for our self-awareness is awakened by other persons and by experiencing objects, all of which therefore become real to us simultaneously with ourselves. If we grew up in complete isolation, we could not develop a human mind and our existence would remain veiled to us in unconsciousness—that is, it would be unknown. Even in the state of developed consciousness our existence remains more mysterious to us than many other experiences; it is more difficult to understand, for instance, than morality. The emphasis on the personal, important as a way of directing our experience, becomes distorted when it is used to isolate the existence of the individual from that of any other person or thing.

The positive side of this emphasis, however, does lead to further valuable insights. The mystery of birth shows that we are unable to choose our existence; it is forced upon us. Nevertheless, to justify the belief in the precedence of existence, the Existentialists must make it in some sense our own choice, and they show convincingly how much of our existence really depends on us. Sartre gives the following example: I may be an invalid without having chosen to be one, but 'I cannot be an invalid . . . without choosing the way in which I regard my infirmity (as "intolerable", "humiliating", "to be concealed", "to be exhibited to all" etc.). I choose myself, not in my being, but in my manner of being.'[1] It is the same, he says, with my past; it seems immutably fixed, but, by the attitude I adopt towards it, I can transform it. This is reminiscent of Kierkegaard's attitude to external characteristics, such as social distinctions, which have to be made meaningful by interpretation, an activity which he helps to explain by his special use of the word 'repetition' in the demand that we should 'repeat' our past constantly, in order to transform it in the light of later experiences and thus give it a constantly increasing meaning.

Yet here, too, the desire to make statements about ultimate reality is an obstacle. The possibility of interpreting one's existence is expressed by Sartre in the following way: 'Man first is—only afterwards is he this or that. Man must create for himself his own essence.' Or, even more clearly: 'Man is not, but makes himself.'[1] He is claiming, in short, that we are not merely developing our personalities by a growing understanding of the different aspects of our human nature, but are creating ourselves, entirely and arbitrarily. But it is evident that our power of choice with regard to our essence is little greater than that with regard to our existence; we act as human beings, whatever we do. We can develop, strengthen and purify the humanity within us, or degrade and almost destroy it, but by no effort can we become, as French critics often say, strawberries or peas or cats.

This error is similar to that of considering reason as absolute, which we have discussed in the first lecture. The Age of Reason disregarded—and all who still cling to it still disregard —the limitations of knowledge; the absolute Existentialists disregard these limitations, too, and, in addition, those of the possible effects of human actions. Because they dismiss reason, they find it even easier to sweep aside all existing limitations to our powers than did those who overestimated reason. A wrong kind of striving for absoluteness must always get away from all real, existing conditions of thinking, feeling and acting; the right kind makes them, like Kierkegaard's, an occasion of an experience of the absolute and a means of guidance in dealing with it. The wrong effort neglects or distorts reality; the right transcends it.

The absolute Existentialists, rebelling against an age which is dominated by determinism, want to establish man's absolute freedom and the assertion that he can create himself is meant to prove this. Sartre insists: 'Dieu n'existe pas', and therefore man is his own master. This emphasis on freedom may be a sound reaction against determinism; but in the long run it does harm to the very freedom which it sets out to defend.

There is no doubt that human freedom is real; we have said before that scientific determinism, even in its psychological form, must not be thought of as superseding it, that we have to start from freedom if we are to understand man.* Though it could, therefore, be of great value to stress freedom, it is a grave mistake to regard it as limitless, for not only is it limited by external conditions (to these we shall return in a moment), but even more by the essence of human existence. Obviously, the concept of freedom must not be allowed to degenerate into that of license or arbitrariness; it should introduce us, as we have seen, to the whole sphere of responsibility, of morality and fundamental values and standards, of trust and love. We shall remain free only if we choose actions which give substance to freedom and increase it; if we merely act as we like, we may succumb to unnoticed compulsions from within or without and thus bury our freedom again. To see freedom as unlimited and thus as undefined makes it meaningless.

Freedom exists for us in two forms which we could call, somewhat paradoxically, 'freedom of choice' and 'choice of freedom'. If we are free, we must be free to choose, but we can make either a choice which really sets us free or a wrong choice which enslaves us again. Freedom could perhaps be best defined as acting entirely by our own free will, but if we are not to be enslaved again, we must also be willing to act in accordance with our true nature, so that it can find its full expression; otherwise we shall find that we are forced into actions which violate that nature. If, for instance, we choose money or power, this choice enslaves us, because it forces us into actions which are contrary to our essential

* See pp. 5–6.

humanity; the more we pursue this choice the more impossible it is for us to give to anything else in our nature other than rudimentary expression. The term 'essence' refers to our true nature; it was defined by Kierkegaard as 'ethical self' and certainly this requires further elaboration, but it is precisely this all-important elaboration which is made impossible if essence is discarded and freedom seen as unlimited—that is, as defying any definition. Thus the absolute Existentialists only acknowledge that we must choose, but not that we also ought to choose the right kind of freedom and action.[1]

Because the term 'existence' includes the historical situation in which we find ourselves, the Existentialists are obliged to pay attention to the external limitations of freedom. For Heidegger, our being is a 'being thrown into an historical situation' which we cannot escape. To safeguard our freedom, we have to accept this situation by our own free will; since we cannot alter it, we have to make it our own by incorporating it in our existence. Again, there is a valuable element in this attitude; we shall waste our energy and perhaps even our lives if we constantly struggle against what cannot be changed; we must base our efforts upon a recognition of what is unchangeable. Yet we must struggle against external compulsions, in order to find out the degree—rarely quite obvious—to which we can change our situation, for otherwise we shall give in too easily to every situation and this would distort our characters. The absolute Existentialists, however, do not struggle in this way. In fact, they do not fully face the historical situation; they assimilate only what is in any case part of their philosophy—namely despair. They project their despair into external reality, as we have said before, and then make the historical situation their own by accepting despair. 'My fear is free, and is a manifestation of freedom, I put all my freedom into my fear, and I have freedom.'[2]

Obviously it is not unreasonable to see the situation between the two wars or at the present moment as desperate. But it is also obvious that the absolute Existentialists fail to do justice to the actual historical situation. We have mentioned before that Heidegger's and Sartre's political decisions are dubious ones; they are also uncertain. Heidegger became a Nazi for a time and later denounced Nazism; Sartre became a communist and later left the party. They did not make the situation their own; they surrendered to it, because their historical judgment lacked any proper foundations. Moreover, most of the absolute Existentialists pay little attention to natural science; Heidegger does, but his statements about it are oracular rather than relevant. One of the most important elements of our present situation is thus left out of consideration.

All these errors are due to a failure to make objectivity serve the subjective method. The Existentialists' contempt for those philosophers who concentrate on essence shows very clearly both the merits of Existentialism in general and the shortcomings of its absolute form. It is true that concentration on essence alone leads to abstraction and thus estranges philosophy from life. This kind of philosophy is rightly attacked; essence has to be combined with existence if it is to come to life. Nevertheless, essence cannot be omitted, for, if it is, existence is left void of any content. It is, after all, plainly wrong to consider man as a completely undefined being, as material which can be transformed into anything; there are reasons why he is called a *human* being, and his humanness can—and must—be made the basis of his endeavours. We are also confronted by an external reality to which we have to adapt our lives and which therefore has to be understood, just as much as the historical situation. If essence disappears, everything concrete which could guide our understanding of existence disappears with it—the characteristics of man, of freedom, of the transcendental, of external reality and even of the historical situation.

Thus it is no cause for surprise that Sartre lands himself in complete nihilism. He is forced to say: 'All existing beings are born for no reason, continue through weakness and die by accident . . . Man is a useless passion. It is meaningless that we are born; it is meaningless that we die.' As Nietzsche correctly foresaw, man without God will strive to become a god himself, but even this has become senseless to Sartre; for him 'human reality is pure effort to become God without there being any basis on which to found this effort, and without there being anything that strives in this way'.[1] As the mere possibility of any content has been denied, nothing can remain but nothingness. Heidegger, similarly, says: 'At the very core of existence, nothingness is dissolving being into nothingness.'[2] It is also dissolving, on this basis, the individual who was to be saved from abstraction. Simone de Beauvoir contemplates, with kafka-esque overtones: 'I look at myself in vain in a mirror, tell myself my own story, I can never grasp myself as an entire object, I experience in myself the emptiness that is myself, I feel that I am not.'[3]

For Heidegger, there also arises the problem of consciousness which, however, leads to the same conclusions. We become aware of the world by becoming conscious of it, and thus Heidegger feels entitled to say that 'being is in the consciousness' and that only this fact makes it possible to 'conceptualize . . . a reality in general'.[4] This may sound, at first sight, like an epistemological statement—that 'the mind knows not things immediately, but only by the intervention of the ideas it has of them'.[5] Yet this impression is misleading; epistemology is dismissed; it is consciousness itself which Heidegger wants to grasp. However, we are only conscious if we are conscious of something; consciousness becomes real by the things of which we are conscious; it cannot be grasped as such. The attempt to do so, therefore, inevitably leads to a conviction of complete nothingness. Sartre is led to conclude: 'In that type of being that is called knowing, the only being that we encounter is that which is perpetually here—the known. The knower does not exist, he cannot be grasped . . . The presence of the known is presence to nothing.'[1] It is no help that, to improve the situation, Sartre tries to depreciate consciousness as well; the issue is only confused when he asserts: 'Conscious deliberation is always faked . . . When I deliberate, the die is already cast . . . The decision has already been taken, by the time the will intervenes.'[2] We may indeed cheat ourselves when we decide what to do—but how could a philosophy ever be developed without conscious deliberation?

Indeed, here is the emptiness which Nietzsche predicted, the void which swallows everything; nothingness is at work, according to Heidegger's dictum, to create more and more nothingness. But is it still that nothingness whose recognition we found valuable because it challenges us to lead an 'authentic life'? This nothingness allows no escape from itself and threatens to destroy the authentic life, too, for it is not the void which we discover when facing our actual situation; far too much of it is of the absolute Existentialist's own making. The extreme conclusions show that we must see the void where it actually exists.

Sartre tries to escape this limitless nothingness; he wants to save man's dignity and to establish his responsibility. We have referred to this attempt before and said that it fails because the transcendental remains excluded.* Since the attempt is desperately sincere, however, the failure is truly pathetic, as Sartre himself admits when he uses it to explain his despair:

* See pp. 88–9.

If a man is not but makes himself, and if in making himself he assumes responsibility for the entire race, if there is no value, nor morality laid down *a priori*, but if, in each case, we must decide alone, without any basis, without guidance, and yet for all, how can we fail to feel anxiety when we have to act? Every one of our acts places at stake the meaning of the world and the place of man in the universe; by each of them, even when we do not intend it, we constitute a scale of universal values; how then can it be supposed that we will not be seized with fear before such a total responsibility?[1]

I have quoted once more at some length, because the passage revealingly disproves the 'ifs' with which Sartre begins. He takes for granted that we can achieve absolute results; because man creates himself, his responsibility is 'total'. But is total responsibility possible? It is hardly convincing that a single individual decides for the 'entire race', 'for all', because each single individual has to decide for himself, as sound Existentialism teaches. Our acts may be so wrong or so outrageous that they endanger for many—or even for a whole society—'the meaning of the world and the place of man in the universe'; but if both meaning and man's place really exist, no single act of a single individual can destroy them. We are certainly responsible to an absolute transcendental reality and absolutely responsible for our own actions, which may include responsibility for other people. But these are absolutes which Sartre does not want to admit and so he replaces them by an external, unlimited absoluteness which, since we are not gods, does not make sense. We may, by our actions, strengthen or weaken what we consider to be the right values, but their acceptance by others and thus their universality does not depend on us.

Moreover, there is nothing in this philosophy to prevent us from changing our minds at any moment and thus invalidating again what our acts seem to imply—nothing, in fact, to prevent total irresponsibility. Sartre also says: 'I am placed in the necessity of choosing myself perpetually'—that is, any choice commits anyone only for a moment. His statements are the moving outcries of despair of a man who recognizes the destructive consequences of his inability to believe in the transcendental, in morality, in values, but he falsifies the actual experience of responsibility by inflated abstract claims. There is either responsibility *and* the transcendental, or there is no responsibility at all.

The springs of Sartre's philosophy and its failure can be clearly discerned in his play *The Flies*. It follows the Greek legend in so far as Clytemnestra has killed Agamemnon, and Orestes must kill her to revenge his father; apart from that, the story is completely transformed. Because Clytemnestra, at the beginning of the play, has not expiated her guilt, the town is punished by being covered with innumerable flies—sordidness is introduced to reinforce our impression of the desperateness of the ordeal. Orestes is only concerned with himself; his main problem is: 'Who am I? I hardly exist.' This expresses the situation of most of the absolute Existentialists; unable to give meaning to their everyday existence (which is hardly possible if one wants absoluteness and denies the absolute), they feel that their lives are insignificant and unreal, and therefore try hard to conjure up some 'great' action. Orestes, too, must do something to become real; he therefore murders his mother, but with the aim not of revenging his father nor of re-establishing justice but only of giving substance to his own life. He states explicitly: 'There is no good and evil . . . My deed was good because I have done it . . . Every man must invent his way.' Thus the guilt of the town is made his own; he steals the guilt from them and departs proudly surrounded by the flies; sordidness is once more needed to confirm that he has a firm hold on reality. He is freed now from the god who guided him towards the murder of his mother, because he has interpreted the deed differently; he has recognized his freedom: 'I am my freedom.' It is freedom from morality; its aim is despair.

The senselessness of this freedom—to murder and to embrace what is disgusting—is clear beyond a doubt. The play was written to encourage the French *Résistance* and it was performed in Paris with great courage, during the Nazi occupation of France. But, as neither good nor evil exist, it could equally well be used to defend any murder committed by the Nazis. The 'reality' of existence is achieved at the cost of destroying all distinctions between the values of different acts.

Heidegger, too, tries to justify the absoluteness of Existentialism,* the dismissal of essence and objectivity, the attempt to make the subjective method all-inclusive—but in a different way; he tries to break down the barriers between the objective and the subjective. Obviously, if the subjective method is the only one which must be applied, nothing must be left outside its scope. Heidegger abolishes any distinction between outside and inside by two procedures: when dealing with 'being', with existence in general, he regards being itself as active and able to provide us with a subjective insight which replaces personal participation; when dealing with the existence of man, he sees external reality from an entirely subjective point of view—so subjective indeed, that we are led rather to think of the distorted present-day meaning of the word 'subjective' than of the subjective method.†

---

* Heidegger has denied that he is an Existentialist, because he is mainly concerned with the ultimate nature of being, with 'fundamental ontology'. Nevertheless, there can hardly be any doubt that his original approach is essentially the same as that of all Existentialism; he has, in fact, deeply influenced (or even brought about) the recent development of this kind of philosophy. For a further discussion of this point see M. Grene: *Heidegger*, London 1957. I am indebted to her for some of the translations used in this chapter.

† See pp. 99-100.

To perform these two processes, Heidegger excels in the invention of new words, which he himself considers as his main merit. (As these new words are hardly translatable, I must apologize if some of the following only reproduce approximately what he has to say, and even that in a way which maltreats the English language.) His efforts throw into relief a difficulty which is common to all Existentialists, from Kierkegaard onwards. Because personal participation is required, the philosophers want to reproduce personal experiences exactly; yet because they are concerned with philosophy, all the private elements of such experiences have to be eliminated. On the one hand, therefore, they overburden their philosophical style with concrete details which are hard to convey as the generally valid statements which this style demands; on the other hand they tend to make these details obscure by leaving out the concrete circumstances under which they occur. Kierkegaard is, to a large extent, successful; some of his works are difficult to read, but as his meaning is clear our efforts to understand them fully are always richly rewarded. Sartre, Gabriel Marcel and others try to overcome this difficulty by conveying their philosophy in novels, plays, diaries—a doubtful way out, for their philosophical content is easily obscured by what may be fiction or irrelevant private experience. Heidegger often tries to solve the problem and make matters easier by interpreting such poets or other thinkers as Hölderlin, Rilke, Nietzsche; this, too, is a doubtful solution, for then it is difficult to decide how far these other writers are being interpreted and how far we are being introduced to Heidegger's own philosophy. He also finds it necessary to coin new words.

We must, however, ask whether these new words give an apparent reality to his thought without referring to anything outside it, or whether they reveal new aspects of reality. To

make existence reveal itself to us, nouns are provided with
new verbs which enable them to be active; nothingness is
destructive and creates nothingness (das Nichts nichtet); the
world makes everything more worldly (die Welt weltet);
existence produces essentiality (das Dasein west). The term
'being' is divided, in order to show us many of its facets;
being itself (Sein), as the basis of everything, is distinguished
from actual existence (Dasein), from existing in a particular
way (Sosein), from that which exists in particular forms (das
Seiende) or in a worldly form (In-der-Welt-sein), and so on.
The result is, briefly, as follows: Being itself is hidden by that
which exists, and as we are constantly confronted with
existing things, the problem arises: how can we perceive
being itself, especially as the world makes everything constantly more worldly? Here nothingness, rather surprisingly,
performs a positive task; by destroying that which exists, the
actually existing things, it produces a 'clearing' through the
wood of these things and in this clearing existence can lay
bare essentiality and reveal itself.* Existence, as we have said,
is providing us—with the help of nothingness—with ultimate
insight.

I hope that this brief summary is sufficient to show that
the attempt to break down the barrier between what is
objective and what subjective is futile. There is no doubt that
existence is one (to this we shall return presently). This oneness
can be embodied in works of art—in poems, paintings, music;
it can be experienced and clearly mystics experience it more

---

* Some of the terms defining being show the influence of Hegel. Kierkegaard had
to attack Hegel when he created Existentialism; now that Existentialism has become
absolute, the absoluteness of Hegel, though different, comes back—both Heidegger
and Hegel represent an extreme development of thought; les extrêmes se touchent.
The term 'essentiality', for instance, is meant to be utterly different from 'essence'—
it implies significance and the opposite of superficiality—yet it is derived (in German
as well as in English) from the same word as essence, and if there is essence, it must
needs be essential.

fully than others; but once we grasp reality with the help of thought, we are inevitably confronted with the contrast between objectivity and subjectivity. Guardini, for instance, despite his admiration for Heidegger, makes this very clear when he says: '*Here* am I, and *there* is everything else—this distinction we shall never be able to transcend.' Whenever we try to know something, the difference between the knower and the known is bound to arise; no way of thinking can abolish it. The absolute Existentialists in general, and Heidegger in particular, try to make philosophy do what only literature could do. The unity of existence can be experienced when a work of art or the evocative language of poetry appeal to our feelings, but it cannot be expressed in philosophical or abstract terms.

When Heidegger finally tries to define 'being' directly, he fails, for he defines it as 'constant presentness' and varies this definition in several ways.[1] This is a purely formal definition and does not say what being really is. He therefore concludes by quoting a few lines from a poem of Hölderlin★ which, by their beauty, awaken a strong feeling and thus cover up the emptiness of the actual definition and the wrongness of the attempt to make existence provide us with ultimate knowledge. Reliance on poetry in philosophy—or on plays and novels— can easily be a way of hiding confusing, unwarranted or inconclusive assertions.

One example may be sufficient to illustrate that the unity of existence, though beyond doubt, cannot be grasped directly. Under the influence of absolute Existentialism, many have been led to despise the traditional distinction between body and mind (which was accepted by both Pascal and Kierkegaard), and they support their argument by reference

★ 'Denn es hasset/Der sinnende Gott/Unzeitiges Wachstum.' (For God in his brooding hates untimely growth.)

to recent developments in biology and psychology. Now it would certainly be wrong to doubt that body and mind are one, two aspects of a unity; it is obvious, for instance, that damage to the brain affects our intellectual capabilities. But we are unable adequately to discuss both mental and physical processes at the same time, because we cannot think in terms which are simultaneously adequate to both; we are obliged to consider either the body or the mind. Even if we knew exactly (as scientists hope we shall) which movements of particles in the brain, which electrical impulses and mechanical transmissions of code messages, are produced by every thought, we should still not understand the meaning of the merest fragment of thought. External motion (which can be measured and expressed in mathematical formulae) and the content, the meaning of a thought or sentence (which can only be understood and expressed in the language of words), though two aspects of the same process, are so entirely different that it is impossible to deal with them in the same way. We have to choose between concentrating on material processes, in which case our mind is simply an instrument to which we pay no attention as such, and concentrating on the experiences of our minds, in which case material processes, though they still go on taking place, are neither observed nor described. We have shown in the first chapter that neither biology nor psychology can cross this barrier; if we want to understand both body and mind, nothing can save us from the need to employ two different ways of thinking. There is no third way of thinking which would allow us to grasp their unity by grasping both at the same time.

Heidegger himself confirms these conclusions, despite his opposite intentions, when he approaches reality from the subjective side. Here the all-inclusive unity—which seemed to be established when objective existence gave us subjective insight—completely disappears. We are not confronted with existence as such, with the one-ness of objective and subjective, but with a quite different view, for Heidegger now establishes three other aspects of being—facticity, existentiality and forfeiture.[1]

Facticity we have in part discussed; by it he means that we find ourselves 'thrown into' an historical situation and a world which we cannot choose. But this 'being-in-the-world' is not seen by Heidegger as enabling us to grasp the world as such; the world exists mainly to be 'at hand' for us, 'to be handled'; it is 'stuff' for our use. The possibility of interpreting facts, which Sartre emphasized, now even determines existence itself. In other words: it is an intensely personal facticity; the individual faces the world in his own way and in isolation. The world as it is objectively given is no longer included, nor are human relationships.

Existentiality is what, in his view, indicates our task. As the world is 'stuff at hand', we can make the situation in which we find ourselves entirely our own, can make it our own 'design'. We can transcend ourselves and all given facts by handling the world correctly, and thus break through to ultimate being, to absolute existence. This is what we ought to do; existence no longer does it for us; we should achieve 'essentiality'.

Forfeiture, however, is the great obstacle. We are part of the crowd and tend to betray ourselves by living in the same superficial way as everybody else—an indifferent life on a low level. It is only here that, for Heidegger, human relationships enter; he pays attention only to their negative aspect.

Our individual task is thus more clearly defined; to escape the danger of forfeiture, which is an all-important task, we have to live an authentic life, in accordance with what is essential in our nature. This is to be done by linking facticity with existentiality as closely as possible. The strongest link between the two, as Heidegger sees it, is the passage of time in our lives; since it cannot be reversed, nor lost time regained, it challenges us most strongly to make proper use of our lives. At the end of our lives we are faced with death; therefore we should be constantly aware of it. By making it authentic, too—that is, by dying, not without being prepared for it or indifferently, but consciously in our own way, by experiencing it fully as part of our individual lives—our existence will be made entirely 'essential' and meaningful. This means, however, that *Angst* or *Sorge* (worried care) must become the basic states of our minds; we must accept that it is possible to live essentially only if we accept the state of dread as the fundamental condition of our existence. Subjectivity has come to reign supreme.

In both of Heidegger's attempts—to make existence active, so that it can reveal its meaning to us, and to make us give meaning to existence—the value of the Existentialist approach can again be seen. On the one hand, the distinction which he makes between several aspects of existence gives greater reality and depth to this rather too general term; on the other hand, the demand that we should lead an authentic life gains greater force by being connected with the challenge of time and by taking account of death. Since time once lost is finally wasted and cannot be regained, the passage of time really demands that we should give significance to any fraction of it; and as death is truly and entirely an experience of our own, an experience which cannot be shared, it should be faced in our own way. Complacency and superficiality are left no hiding place.

Yet Heidegger's approach also considerably increases the dangers which arise when Existentialism is made absolute. If nothingness performs a positive task, we are no longer forced

—or even entitled—to fight against it; we must simply contemplate it and wait for it to disclose meaning. This even endangers the authentic life which is elsewhere demanded. For both existence and nothingness come to be endowed with an activity of their own which personifies them and virtually makes them something like gods—that is, they acquire a mystical quality which, as we have mentioned before, cannot be genuine once the transcendental has been denied. There is hardly anything more dangerous than the endowing of things or concepts with mystical qualities, since this gives them an exaggerated importance which makes men willing to kill for their sake. Nietzsche, when creating the superman, raised such concepts as 'race' and 'earth' to this false mystical level; the Nazis extended this to such concepts as 'blood', 'nordic' and many others; Heidegger, being prone to do the same, succumbed to Nazism. For him, as for Sartre, there is no 'morality given a *priori*', in fact no morality at all; some new god may come into being in the distant future, but at present 'dieu n'existe pas'. Yet Existentialism, by concentrating upon inner experience, leads us to the transcendental, which, if it is not admitted, has to be replaced. But, since all these replacements increase the power of destructive nothingness, absolute Existentialism helps us to recognize that absoluteness must be sought precisely in that region whose existence Sartre and Heidegger deny—in the region of the transcendental.

Authentic life is also undermined by Heidegger's isolation of the individual. His 'facticity', as we have said, is entirely subjective, so subjective that it does not even include personal relationships. He never shows any understanding of such relationships, he is simply not concerned with them; they are only considered when he discusses 'forfeiture'—that is, as completely negative. Man, however, does not live in isolation, so that Heidegger's representation of him must remain artificial and misleading. *Angst* and *Sorge*, by themselves, are no substitute for what he omits; combined with the isolation of the individual, they bar the way to other basic feelings, such as the love of one's neighbour, the deep satisfaction aroused by goodness, the inner certainty of faith, all of which require that due weight should be given to positive human relationships and to the transcendental. Nor can the emphasis on an authentic death, if it does not point beyond itself, solve the problem of the absolute; such a death confronts us with a nothingness which can be no more than senseless destruction.

That contemporary Existentialism need not be absolute and thus destructive is shown clearly by Jaspers. He emphasizes the experience of what he calls 'boundary situations'. This means that he, too, emphasizes death, despair and nothingness, but he also takes into account other experiences, such as illness and, especially, guilt. He sees man more objectively and is concerned with morality and with human relationships. He is aware of the limitations of knowledge and deals, therefore, with 'the problem of communication', with the question, that is, of how knowledge of the transcendental, even though it can be neither directly expressed nor shown as the result of a conscious effort of thought, could nevertheless be communicated to others. By this widening of the scope of philosophy he can give to the negative experiences (which he faces just as unreservedly as Sartre and Heidegger) a positive significance.

He wants us to seek extreme boundary situations, or at least not to disregard those which are, in any case, unavoidable. He sees that in so doing we shall be aware of our failure to cope with them and that we may break down. Before we experience them, however, we shall also expect to be confronted with meaningless nothingness, with complete despair.

But he shows that to face failure in those boundary situations which are beyond our strength is more important than any success. For, when it is experienced, nothingness gives way to something different—we are confronted by a reality which transcends and comprehends our existence, a reality larger than ourselves. However far we extend the scope of our experience—even if we go to the farthest boundaries we can ever reach—there is always something beyond, something positive which comes to our rescue at the very moment when we seem lost. For Jaspers as for Kierkegaard, despair removes the deceptive apparent certainties on which we are wont to rely and confronts us with the most basic certainty—with an absolute reality which points towards religion. Apparently we fail, and there seems to be nothing left but despair and nothingness; yet in fact we are led to discover the fullness of existence.

As Jaspers, however, still overemphasizes the negative boundary situations and pays insufficient attention to those positive experiences of the same order which we have mentioned before—such as strong experiences of love or of the good—I want to turn to Buber, so as to be able to show some further positive aspects of Existentialism.

CHAPTER VIII

PERSONAL RELATIONSHIPS—
MARTIN BUBER

The desire for some kind of absoluteness—even though, as we have seen, it tends to lead astray both those who still cling to some of the claims of the Age of Reason and the extreme Existentialists—is fundamentally justified, for we experience our own existence with absolute certainty. There have been attempts by philosophers throughout the ages to question even this fact, but they have proved futile. We know beyond any doubt that we exist.

This absolute knowledge represents a challenge. It makes intuitively accessible only an unexplained fact, and we naturally want to know more; we want to have an equally absolute knowledge of the foundations and the meaning of our existence. But the frequent failures of attempts to establish absolute knowledge show that we must look for it in the right direction.

We have to pay attention to the limitations of any knowledge which we can possibly gain—that is, to the fact that there is no knowledge which is both comprehensive and absolute. (As before, by knowledge in this context I mean a knowledge achieved by a conscious effort of thinking.) The objective method can lead, as the natural sciences show, to knowledge which includes the whole of external reality and even man, so far as he can be understood from outside; it may become very nearly comprehensive. But to be objective, the method has, as far as is humanly possible, to exclude the observer, and thus to accept certain presupposed conditions;

therefore, as we have seen in the first chapter, knowledge achieved in this way is relative and not absolute. The question 'Why?' cannot be answered, on this basis, in any fundamental sense, nor can man's inner experiences be included. The subjective method, on the other hand, can lead to the transformation of single experiences into an access to absolute knowledge, but as the absoluteness is an integral part of the actual experience, this knowledge cannot be used as a basis for generalizations and is not comprehensive. It can never justify, for instance, such statements as 'The universe is good,' because we are unable to experience the whole universe. To achieve absolute knowledge we must therefore renounce comprehensiveness and choose those inner experiences which, with the help of the subjective method, promise to yield relevant results.

Martin Buber chooses personal relationships, and his choice proves particularly fruitful. We have mentioned that one of the most promising signs of present-day philosophy is to be found in those forms of Existentialism which put at its centre, not an abstract mind considering the universe, but man among men.* This should be a natural tendency in Existentialism, but some Existentialists, as we have seen in the preceding chapter, do isolate man again; others, however, such as Jaspers, pay attention to the problem of communication, but none more successfully than Buber.

His main work dealing with this problem is the book *I and Thou*. This book gives further support to our contention that the relationship between cause and effect cannot easily be detected in human affairs and that books can, in the long run, have an unpredictable influence.† *I and Thou* is a small book, written in 1922, in the Expressionist style then prevalent in Germany, which means that the style is half-mystical and ecstatic, often hiding the thought rather than disclosing it, a

* See p. 99.　　　† See pp. 66-7.

failing which, as will be seen in some of the following quotations, becomes even more obvious in translation. Yet this book has, especially in this country, had a greater influence upon philosophy and theology than many a large and well-written work; the phrase 'I and Thou' has become generally accepted as the name of those factors in human experience which Buber describes.

He distinguishes between two kinds of fundamental relationships which he calls '*I–It*' and '*I–Thou*'. This is based on his claim that, whenever we say the word '*I*', we really never consider ourselves in isolation; we either establish a relationship with objects or other persons seen from outside (the '*It*' can be replaced by '*He*' or '*She*'), or we enter into the personal relationship indicated by *I–Thou*. This corresponds roughly to our distinction between the objective and subjective methods, but it helps considerably to clarify this distinction and to elaborate further the subjective method.

'The primary word *I–It*,' as Buber calls it, 'cannot be said with my whole being.' Because the knowledge thus acquired has to be independent of the observer, the *I* has to exclude certain parts of himself; only certain special faculties are required. On the other hand, 'the primary word *I–Thou* can be spoken only with the whole being.'[1] For the relationship can only arise when the *I* is completely involved, without any reservations, and fully responding to the impact the other person makes upon him.

The nature of this response is made clear by what Buber calls 'a personal meeting'. To experience it, we have to meet another person, not in a conventional or official way, but so that his full response to our approach becomes one of the greatest satisfactions we can have and a lack of response hurts us deeply. We must be so completely absorbed in the meeting that any other consideration disappears. 'When *Thou* is

spoken, the speaker . . . takes his stand in relation', in the immediate relationship to the other, and by his experience he is enabled to confirm: 'All real living is meeting' (pp. 4, 11).*
What Buber has in mind can perhaps be explained by a comparison between reading a book, listening to a lecture, and having a conversation. When we read a book, its author makes his impact upon us; yet our thoughts can wander, we can be distracted, interrupt the reading and take it up again, and we can fall asleep while reading. Therefore, as we are not completely involved, this is not yet a meeting in Buber's sense. When we listen to a lecture, our personal relationship with the lecturer may play a greater part, but our thoughts can still wander and we can still fall asleep. In a conversation, however, if it is to be a true conversation, we obviously have to be present and attentive all the time. If we do not listen, we shall not be able to answer, nor to hold the attention of our partner. We must really try to understand and to make ourselves understood, try to convince and to allow ourselves to be convinced; the conversation will be at its best if we do not make any reservations—if we neither hide our true opinions nor endeavour to refute our partner at all costs, but react fully in an honest and open-minded way. Otherwise either we ourselves or our partner will be in the position of Queen Victoria, disliking Gladstone because he addressed her like a public meeting. When, however, we succeed in making and eliciting a complete and frank response, we experience the personal meeting which Buber demands. We must neither want, nor be able, to escape.

The emphasis on such a meeting is in agreement with Existentialist philosophy; nevertheless, the difference between the extreme Existentialists and Buber is striking. For them,

* Page numbers in parentheses on this and the following pages refer to *I and Thou*.

man's existence is suspended between two poles of nothingness —between that before birth and that after death. For Buber, the personal meeting is the middle stage between two other kinds of meetings, both of which are positive. The first stage he calls 'life with nature', for we do not approach things only in the objective *I-It* way, we can also experience them and be educated by them; they can give rise to inner experiences. This stage can be felt, but not fully expressed (except in works of art, to which we shall return later), because the response is one-sided. The third stage is 'life with the spiritual'; here we can feel the relationship, it can lead to intuition and inspiration, and if it does we can in good moments also express it. Here we are being addressed, but addressed by a partner who transcends us so immensely that an articulate response will only be possible in moments of great inner strength. The middle stage, 'life with men' (p. 6), is safely rooted between these two other stages, and it is this stage which can be fully expressed by language, because language can make claims on the other person and evoke a full response. Buber first concentrates on the personal meeting, therefore, but this can lead on, as it cannot in the teachings of the extreme Existentialists, to a giving of substance to the transcendental, and it can do this more directly even than by Kierkegaard's approach.

The personal meeting is based on the experience of the *Thou*, and Buber explains this experience with the help of the doctrines of the 'Gestalt' or 'configuration' school of psychology. Followers of this school claim, for instance, that we do not see first one tree, then two trees, then more trees, and then conclude that there is a forest, but that the forest is our first impression, and that only afterwards do we analyse it into the seeing of many trees. Similarly, when listening to music, we do not take in one note after the other and then recognize the melody, but the melody is heard first, and the awareness of the single notes needs an additional effort. Any experienced reader will confirm that he does not read one letter after the other, but sees words or even sequences of words as an immediate whole, as a configuration. It is in this way that, in a meeting, we get an intuitive impression of the whole person that we meet. As Buber says: 'Just as the melody is not made up of notes nor the verse of words nor the statue of lines . . . so with the man to whom I say *Thou*. I can take out from him the colour of his hair, or of his speech, or of his goodness. I must continually do this. But each time I do it he ceases to be *Thou*' (pp. 8–9). To experience the *Thou* means to have an immediate knowledge of the whole man.

The meeting takes place through grace. By pointing this out, Buber makes the difficult concept 'grace' more easily accessible, which in its turn further elucidates the experience of a meeting. Buber shows the roots of grace in everyday life, and even though this kind of grace must not be identified with what it means for the Christian, it also helps to make more comprehensible the Christian concept of grace. We can actually see the working of grace in many different contexts. We cannot make ourselves appreciate the beauty of, say, a poem; it may 'reveal' its beauty to us once or never, or we may read it many times without full understanding and then suddenly understand it. We may try hard to act in accordance with the moral law and feel nothing but the strain of so doing, until the experience of goodness in another person brings the moral law to life and we realize what we have previously missed. None of our endeavours can directly produce final understanding of the poem or of goodness; understanding is pure 'grace'. Certainly, we have to be willing to respond to such an experience, to accept it, to live through it; otherwise it will pass unnoticed or have no consequences. We need, as we have said, personal participation. But even the will to participate is not of itself sufficient to make participation possible. We have to strive, yet none of our endeavours can guarantee the attainment of what we seek; we have to knock at the door, but it has to be opened for us. All this is seen most clearly in a personal meeting: 'The *Thou* meets me through grace—it is not found by seeking . . . The *Thou* meets me. But *I* step into direct relation with it. Hence the relation means being chosen and choosing' (p. 11). We have to be active and receptive at the same time; our striving is necessary, but the successful meeting is not simply its consequence.

Two points are of special importance here. On the one hand, the term 'grace' gives a much more adequate account of the interconnexion between intention and result in the purely personal sphere than any explanation in terms of cause and effect. To be ready for such a meeting, we have to forget about causality: 'So long as the heaven of *Thou* is spread out over me the winds of causality cower at my heels, and the whirlpool of fate stays its course' (p. 9). On the other hand, as we have to be both active and receptive, the meeting is 'suffering and action in one', and this applies to any action in which we are completely involved: 'Any action of the whole being, which means the suspension of all partial actions and consequently of all sensations of actions grounded only in their particular limitation, is bound to resemble suffering'* (p. 11). Reliance on grace might encourage inactivity, passive waiting, or even laziness, a misunderstanding against which both St Paul and Luther had to struggle once they had established man's complete dependence on grace. The *I–Thou* relationship makes it clear that, in this realm, no such distinction between activity and passivity can be made; nor can

---

* In German the word 'Leiden' means both being passive and experiencing suffering. Thus for Buber the word 'suffering' always implies both meanings.

suffering be avoided. In this it is, after all, similar to Kierkegaard's 'leap into the unknown', which is both passive acceptance and an action, and which is bound to involve us in suffering.

At the same time, we are enabled to experience the present. This is a difficult and essential task. As long as we are pre-occupied with practical life, we are determined by the past upon which we must build, and we are constantly planning for the future; the present is a barely perceptible dividing line where the future incessantly slips back into the past. Yet obviously, if our experience is to be a full one, we must live in the present, give it content and duration, concentrate on what we actually experience, without paying attention to the passage of time. This is the condition, for example, of a good conversation, and it is achieved in the personal meeting. 'The real, filled present exists only in so far as actual presentness, meeting, and relation exist. The present arises only in virtue of the fact that the *Thou* becomes present . . . It is your present; only while you have it you have the present' (pp. 12, 33). We can really live a full life.

A work of art can fulfil the same function. For Buber describes the artist, in the widest sense of the word, as a man for whom the subject of his representation has become a *Thou*; and we, when appreciating the work of art, must make this work a *Thou* for us, in order to experience its full impact. The *I–Thou* relationship is at work here, too.

This does not mean that the objective method is excluded. We need both the subjective and the objective methods, because of what Buber calls the 'exalted melancholy of our fate'—that we cannot constantly live in the *I–Thou* relationship, nor live constantly in the present. 'Every *Thou* in our world must become an *It*. It does not matter how exclusively present the *Thou* was in the direct relation. As soon as the relation has been worked out or has been permeated with a means, the *Thou* becomes an object among objects . . . Love itself cannot persist in direct relation. It endures, but in interchange of actual and potential being' (pp. 16–17). Or: 'It is not possible to live in the bare present. Life would be quite consumed if precautions were not taken to subdue the present speedily and thoroughly.' The objective method, therefore, is necessary, but Buber's emphasis is on seeing its limitations and on making us aware of the indispensable subjective method: 'It is possible to live in the bare past, indeed only in it a life may be organized. We only need to fill each moment with using, and it ceases to burn . . . Without *It* man cannot live. But he who lives with *It* alone is not a man' (p. 34).

The difficulty is that the *I–Thou* world can be neither generalized nor kept in being by some kind of order; the *Thou* is evanescent; because it cannot last, it has constantly to be experienced anew. Experiencing the *Thou* means grasping something objective which cannot be reproduced by abstractions, but which only becomes accessible in experience; when we want to hold it, it escapes, when we want to survey it, we lose it, for it becomes an *It*. No metaphysical system, no social order can make it permanent, for as soon as it is located within a constant framework, as a stable object of knowledge, it loses its distinctive character. Ideas may help to re-create the experience, but they are no substitute, for they also belong to the world of the *It*.

Nevertheless, to know of the experience of the *Thou* is essential. It is when he discusses order and organization that Buber says: 'A world that is ordered is not the world-order' (p. 31). This was said long before the nature of modern totalitarianism was understood (which was not when it was established in Russia, but only after the advent of fascism and Nazism). A dictatorial bureaucracy can so easily give the satisfying impression that, at long last, order has been established, and yet it may be the result of chaos. The experience of the *Thou*, even though not grasped as part of a social organization, keeps us aware of the conditions which a human community should fulfil.

In fact, there is a kind of knowledge which is based on the awareness of the *I–Thou* relationship and its constantly renewed experience—on its 'potentiality and actuality'. It cannot be systematized, but it can gradually accumulate. Our discussion so far has shown that we can get to know the conditions of the relationship more clearly, which will obviously help us to renew it, to experience and understand it more fully, and this can bear fruit because there is a centre where the accumulation can take place as a focus of growth—the knowledge of our own personality.

The main effect of the personal meeting is that we ourselves are forced into the open; we learn more about ourselves than on any other occasion and more than we can about the other person. We have mentioned that we acquire an intuitive knowledge of this other man, not of his particular characteristics (which would make him an *It*) but of his whole personality. The same happens to our knowledge of ourselves; we learn to distinguish between what is merely characteristic of the individual which we accidentally happen to be, and our human nature—that within us which is common to all men. Buber's words are: 'If we go on our way and meet a man who has advanced towards us and has also gone on his way, we know only our part of the way, not his—his we experience only in the meeting. Of the complete relational event we know, with the knowledge of life lived, our going out to the relation, our part of the way. The other part only comes upon us, we do not know it; it comes upon us in the meeting . . . The *Thou* confronts me. The *I* steps into direct relation with it' (p. 76).

In this context Buber introduces another important distinction—that between 'individuality' and 'person'. Individuality is that in us which makes us different from others; but there is also the common ground on which the *I–Thou* meeting takes place. 'Individuality makes its appearance by being differentiated from other individualities. A person makes his appearance by entering into relation with other persons. The one is the spiritual form of natural detachment, the other the spiritual form of natural solidarity of connexion' (p. 62). Individuality includes character, race, activity, profession, even genius.* The person represents what Buber calls 'selfhood' and it is expressed by the statement 'I am' and not by 'I am thus'. The *I–Thou* relationship is concerned with the person, but to understand it we have to be aware both of our individuality and of our person, and it is this awareness which the personal meeting helps to produce.

This distinction removes a difficulty which has baffled many philosophers. It is often expressed by asking: 'How do I know that other minds exist?' If this question is answered by those who rely on the objective method, the answer is that we observe other persons acting, reacting and behaving like ourselves, speaking a language we can understand, and it is the enumeration of such single observations which finally leads to the conclusion that other persons may probably have what, within ourselves, we call 'mind'. We need only remember what we have said about 'Gestalt'-psychology to recognize that this is not how our minds work.† The extreme Existentialists claim that we know only our own existence; they thus cut themselves off from the knowledge of others, and then desperately try to account for, and establish human relationships. Their attempt must needs remain futile. Buber

* Buber's position is here the same as Kierkegaard's; see p. 68.
† See pp. 143–4.

insists that the *I* and the *Thou* grow together; 'through the *Thou* a man becomes *I*' (p. 28). It is the meeting with other minds which produces the growth of our own mind; if we grew up in complete isolation we could not develop a human mind at all, a fact which has been confirmed by reports about children growing up among wild animals. Therefore, we really know first that other minds exist, and only through their impact upon us do we become aware of our own minds. The person is not an isolated entity.

Buber tries to convey the nature of the common bond between men by clarifying the concept of 'love', of that love which he defines as 'the responsibility of an *I* for a *Thou*' (p. 15), the equivalent of love of one's neighbour. He emphasizes that this love exists *between* two persons who meet, not just inside each of them—that there actually is something in existence between them. This may sound strange at first, because Buber uses the spatial term 'between' for a feeling which cannot be of a spatial nature, but he wants to stress once more that 'to step into relation' is essential. It is not enough to see each man as a separate vessel of feeling; the *I* plus a feeling, however temptingly laudable the feeling may be, does not yet constitute a person in his sense of the word, nor does the individual feeling as such yet represent true love. This emphasis is, in fact, a good antidote against any complacent indulgence in feelings against sentimentality and weak pity; it is not sufficient that I feel; my love must go out towards the other person, so that, even if it remains one-sided, it must be 'action and suffering in one.' But it becomes fully real when the two persons thus meet on common ground.

This meeting on common ground has important political and religious implications.

If the *I* remains a separate vessel of feeling, social aspirations do not yet create a community which should, after all, be our aim; even socialism with a certain amount of private feeling added to it remains insufficient. To show the need of the *I–Thou* relationship even for society, Buber introduces, in another book, the concept '*We*'.[1] He claims that because we lack the awareness of the *We*, our society is caught between two wrong extremes—between modern individualism and modern collectivism. 'Both views—however different others of their causes and expressions may be—are essentially the result of the same situation, only at different stages of development. It is a situation due to the combination of cosmic and social homelessness, to a fear of the world and life, characterized by such loneliness as was probably never experienced before. Each human being feels himself cut off, as man, from nature, and isolated, as a person, in the middle of swarming masses. His first reaction to the recognition of this new and uncanny situation is modern individualism, the second is modern collectivism . . . If, however, individualism, grasps only part of man, collectivism sees man only as a part; both miss the whole man, man in his wholeness. Individualism perceives man only in his relationship with himself; collectivism does not see man at all, but only society. The former distorts the face of man, the latter covers and hides it.' The answer is the *We*—'a community of a definite number of independent persons who know selfhood and responsibility', who are living in the *I–Thou* relationship, or at least experiencing it from time to time. A true community must be built upon the faculty of man to say *Thou*.

This may sound as Utopian as Kierkegaard's political demands; yet once again it agrees with our actual experience. Is there any starting point which provides hope unless we ourselves begin to recognize, to experience, to aim at the *We* within the context of society? The revival of real communities within the masses is obviously essential if society is to become a world of persons.

At the same time, love, disclosing the common ground between men, discloses a higher, a spiritual reality. We have, in discussing Kierkegaard's views, already said that love shows the breaking into our existence of something transcendental,* and the results at which Buber arrives are, like Kierkegaard's, very similar to the Christian assertion that the fatherhood of God is the condition of the brotherhood of men. But Buber is no Christian; he arrives at these results in a different way which, by being more direct than any other, also elucidates the Christian doctrine of love.

The fact that, in a personal meeting, the other addresses me and that I can be addressed, that I see in him also the person who I am, indicates, as we have just said, that we meet on common ground. This common ground cannot be our human nature alone, for it is experienced as an 'inescapable claim'†—that is, it reveals something absolute which addresses every man. We are, according to Buber, addressed by what he calls the 'final *Thou*'—a *Thou* which cannot become an *It*, because it transcends immensely all our knowledge; we know it only through being addressed. This final *Thou* is the basis of every human *Thou*; it enables us to experience a personal meeting, for by being addressed we ourselves are constantly (even if often only potentially) in the state of being the *Thou*. In other words: God, by addressing us, sets us free to experience the *I–Thou* relationship with men; the personal meeting discloses God as its common ground, and thus God becomes a real experience in the *I–Thou* relationship. A relationship which we actually experience becomes possible because there is a God.

This fact, however, is also important for the idea of God.

* See pp. 67–8.   † See p. 93.

Since He may 'properly only be addressed, not expressed' (p. 81), one should neither talk about God nor try to define Him. Instead, any concept of God should include the *Thou*, so that we can address him and listen to ourselves being addressed. This approach gives us a greater understanding of the nature of religion; it makes it impossible, for instance, for us to despise primitive religions; because they try to establish faith by making the godhead a *Thou*, they are, however unsatisfactory to us, a step in the right direction. But Buber makes a reservation concerning Buddhism, so as to emphasize that nothing, not even the highest intellectual or moral standards, should be allowed to suppress the *Thou*. The original form of Buddhism was atheistic, so that there was no *Thou* to whom to turn, and as this could not be reconciled with the true function of religion, Buddhism suffered distortion; several of its denominations, contrary to his own intentions, transformed Buddha into a god so as to introduce the *Thou* which could be addressed. No religion can remain pure if it becomes impersonal.

Buber's concept of God, moreover, allows the boundaries between philosophy and religion to be clearly defined. 'Instead of including God as one theme among others, that is, as the highest theme of all, philosophy both wholly and in part would be compelled to point toward God, without actually dealing with him. This means that the philosopher would be compelled to recognize and admit the fact that his idea of the Absolute was dissolving at the point where the Absolute lives; that it was dissolving at the point where the Absolute is loved; because at that point the Absolute is no longer the "Absolute" about which one may philosophize, but God.'[1]

The word 'absolute' itself can help us to understand what Buber means. The philosopher who faces experience honestly will be forced to use this adjective, just as we have done. But it indicates, in fact, merely something which has to be recognized as ultimate and underived, and which we must accept as such, without being able to explain it. But we can hardly use it without using the term 'the absolute', and the noun goes one step further; its meaning, however, is still limited to the statement that, in all such experiences as those of absolute values, something more comprehensive is felt which embodies absoluteness, but which can be neither defined nor grasped more directly nor expressed by more definite concepts. At this point we reach the boundaries of knowledge and of philosophy which strives for knowledge. The word indicates this very well, for as we are unable to know the absolute, it remains indefinable and empty, while implying something to be looked for beyond the knowable, just as the word 'boundaries' implies that there is a farther realm which we cannot reach. With religion, however, this is the starting point, because for the believer 'the Absolute' is not empty, but God (or a spiritual reality of some kind) and thus real and full of inexhaustible meaning. The task of the philosopher, therefore, is to show the absolute whenever it is implied in knowledge, in spite of the fact that it transcends philosophy; to show where knowledge points towards the transcendental, even though it cannot deal with it. But philosophy must not include God, who, as Buber says, cannot be expressed. The philosopher cannot, within philosophy, legitimately claim that there is a God (even though many have done so), but he can show the points where, for the believer, faith will have to replace demonstration. If the philosopher respects these boundaries, he can concentrate on metaphysical problems without incurring the danger that Pascal feared—that God would become the god of the philosophers.

The nature of religion is further clarified by Buber's rejection of mysticism, even in its purest form. Pure mysticism aims at an all-inclusive one-ness; the mystic experiences, in moments of ecstasy, a complete union in which God and man are merged. Buber insists that the opposition between *I* and *Thou* remains indispensable even in the sphere of religious experience; as God addresses me, my person remains essential—*I* am saved, *I* am delivered, *I* matter. All mystic discipline presupposes that God is within me; 'but truly though God surrounds us and dwells in us, we never have Him within us' (p. 104). All mysticism treats external reality as merely an illusion, but this reality can—and should—become that stage of the *I–Thou* relationship which Buber calls 'life with nature',* and this should educate us. Mysticism also wants to overcome or even, in some of its forms, to exclude suffering, but as suffering is part of the action in the meeting, it must be at work in the *I–Thou* relationship.

For these reasons, Buber turned away from mysticism, which first attracted him. He acknowledges the mystical experience of unity which he may once have experienced: '*I* and *Thou* are absorbed, humanity, which just before confronted the godhead, is merged in it—glorification, deification, and singleness of being have appeared.' But he rejects this experience because faith should permeate all our life: 'When the man, illuminated and exhausted falls back into the cares of earthly affairs, and with knowledge in his heart thinks of the two situations, is he not bound to find that his being is split asunder and one part given to perdition? What does it help my soul that it can be withdrawn anew from this world here into unity, when this world itself has of necessity no part in the unity—what does all "enjoyment of God" profit a life that is rent in two? If that abundantly rich heavenly moment has nothing to do with my earthly moment—what has it then to do with me, who have still to live, in all seriousness still to live, on earth? Thus are the masters to be under-

* See p. 143.

stood who have renounced the raptures of ecstatic "union"'*
(pp. 86-7). The transcendental can only be valid if it proves to
be the basis of our life here and now, for we know it only
in and through our existence.

Pantheism is rejected on similar grounds. 'God comprises,
but is not, the universe. So, too, God comprises, but is not, my
Self . . . In view of this *I* and *Thou* live, and dialogue and
spirit and language (spirit's primal act) and the Word in
eternity' (p. 95). In both mysticism and pantheism the concept
of God, by being made all-inclusive, endangers the human
person, and thus usually leads to a wrong reaction—to making
the *I* self-centred, cutting it off from other men and the
transcendental altogether. Or, to put it differently and in
Buber's way: we hardly understand the meaning of 'the
Word' in its biblical sense any longer, but know only words;
if we do not experience the creative action of God as the final
Thou, our life is always in danger of being reduced to the level
of the *I–It* relationship.

It is only by the *I–Thou* relationship that we can share in
a true religious revelation. A revelation is true, according to
Buber, when it shows that we are 'accepted' and thus connected with the whole of existence; when it confirms that
this existence has a meaning, and when this meaning makes
our lives of fundamental consequence here and now and not
only in a life hereafter. He always judges religion by how it
deals with this world, producing a criterion which could
help us to evaluate different religions or different denominations
within a religion. But we are estranged from the revelation
because religion develops in three stages. The first, which
we have just described, Buber calls 'living revelation'; it leads
to immediate action; it is the stage of the Ten Commandments.

* This is another reason why Buddhism, with its mystical expectation of an impersonal Nirvana, is rejected.

Later the forms of religion are emphasized, yet these forms are effective; this is the stage of the creation of the church and ritual; it is still alive, but is beginning to move towards the *It*. Finally, religion is only 'valid'—that is, taken as an accepted truth and thus no more than an abstract doctrine; at this stage we have only words instead of the Word. Once this stage is reached, there is no other way of regaining the living revelation, of making religion part of our lives, but the experience of the *I–Thou* relationship—with men and with God.

This view could perhaps remove a great obstacle to modern man's attempt to accept Christianity—to see Christ as the centre of history. We have become so accustomed to historical thinking, to the theory of evolution, even to belief in progress, that we are bound to see history as a constant development. How can it be centred, then, on an event which happened in the remote past? It must seem to us to have been superseded, long ago, by all that has happened since. But if we fully experience the *I–Thou* relationship, it becomes the centre of our lives and all experiences are related to it; we constantly refer to it, even by transforming past experiences in its light; it elucidates the meaning of the whole of existence or gives meaning to it for the first time. Our experiences become, as it were, transparent.[1] Even a single personal meeting can become a centre of great importance; how much more powerful must such a centre be if God is met as a *Thou*! Christ, for Buber, knew the *Thou* best; once we meet him as *Thou*, he will become the centre to which all history must be related.

Buber is not a Christian, but emphatically a Jew; he speaks of Jesus, not of Christ. He accepts Jesus as probably the greatest of the prophets, but not as mediator, not as the son of God. He objects to giving God a name and wants no more than God's answer to Moses: 'I am who I am.' Yet it is probably no accident that Buber has exercised such a profound influence upon Christian theologians: to re-live, to renew Christianity, many may have to pass once again through the stage of Judaism, of the Old Testament. The direct impact of a nameless God perhaps presents fewer difficulties to modern man than Christianity; it may also remove some of the too anthropomorphic images of God (which seem emptier to the outsider than to the believer) and thus help to restore to Christianity that majesty which Nietzsche found lacking and for which Kierkegaard struggled. It may also enable us to accept the final emphasis of Buber's investigation—that the aim is not, as in science, the solution of problems, but reconciliation and salvation.

There is one point, however, which Buber does not discuss —any derivation of the *I–Thou* relationship itself from any more fundamental experience; it is accepted as ultimate and absolute. I hope that our discussion has shown how fruitful this assumption is, and now that we have understood what this relationship means we can add that it is also fully justified. The *I–Thou* is obviously more basic than the *I–It*, for the *It* must exclude the person (in Buber's sense of the word) and the transcendental and is thus arrived at by abstraction and simplification, while the *Thou* which is based on the person and the transcendental can nevertheless include nature and the external world. Once we have truly met a person, moreover, all the relative elements of individuality become unimportant, thus confirming that it is the person which is basic to our existence. As Macmurray says: 'It is just nonsense to say that people of different races, or different professions, or different nationalities, or different sexes, cannot be friends. Of course they can, and are. Personal relationships override all the distinctions which differentiate people. Personal relationship is possible between any two persons because it is based purely on the fact that they are both persons.'[1]

The absoluteness which Buber thus establishes is 'existential', but it is very different from what we have called 'absolute Existentialism'. He sees clearly the mistakes of that philosophy; talking about Sartre and Heidegger, for instance, he says: 'Of the two who have taken up Nietzsche's expression of the death of God, one, Sartre, has brought it and himself *ad absurdum* through his postulate of the free invention of meaning and value. The other, Heidegger, creates a concept of rebirth of God out of the thought of truth which falls into the enticing net of historical time,'[1] thus cutting himself off from the transcendental which alone could lead to such a rebirth. Therefore, both must remain destructive, which is exactly the opposite of what Buber achieves.

Buber seems similar to the prophets of gloom when he comes to the diagnosis of our own time; he describes the void which threatens us in an even more terrifying way, perhaps, than they do. For he, as we have seen, the *I–Thou* and the *I–It* relationship 'build up human existence'; therefore 'it is only a question of which of the two is at any particular time the architect and which is his assistant. Rather, it is a question of whether the *I–Thou* relation remains the architect, for it is self-evident that it cannot be employed as assistant. If it does not command, then it is already disappearing. In our age the *I–It* relation, gigantically swollen, has usurped, practically uncontested, the mastery and the rule. The *I* of this relation, an *I* that possesses all, makes all, succeeds with all, this *I* is unable to say *Thou*, unable to meet a being essentially ... (It) can naturally acknowledge neither God nor any genuine absolute which manifests itself to men as of non-human origin. It steps in between and shuts off from us the light of heaven.'[2]

To a large extent, this diagnosis is certainly justified and it may sound desperate, but heaven is not finally closed to us. The power of the *I–It*, seen in this way, is a challenge to the

I-Thou, and every experience of a personal meeting, which can be more clearly understood in the light of this belief, will become a step away from destruction towards a meaningful life. Such meetings, moreover, cannot be entirely prevented. Here is the counterweight to nothingness which all Existentialists found necessary, but which Nietzsche, Sartre and Heidegger failed to create. We have to admit experience as evidence; but if experience is seen in all its depth, Existentialism will lead, as our discussion of Kierkegaard also showed, to those results we were looking for—to positive results which we are entitled to accept.

In addition, Buber's approach has another very important merit. He does not only offer a discussion of personal relationships which, once his terminology is understood, is probably more helpful than most others; he has discovered a way in which we can speak meaningfully about what is so often vaguely or contemptuously called 'mystical'. The transcendental, a religious experience, the supernatural or divine reality, God—everything which these concepts try to indicate is extremely difficult to discuss, the more so as our age has become so uncertain about anything spiritual that words which defy any definition seem in particular need of it. Buber enables us to discuss the transcendental in terms of everyday experience which we can test for ourselves, and even to distinguish between genuine experiences of the divine and misleading kinds of mysticism. His approach is neither abstract nor for the initiated only; few will deny that at least the first stages of his argument make sense. Thus, however, he can enable those who have an experience of the divine to relate it to experiences which are common to all men, and this may lead to the recognition of the final *Thou* which, as Buber claims, creates this common ground by addressing us. God will no longer remain hidden, but speak to us again.

CHAPTER IX

THE IRRATIONAL IN SCIENCE AND RELIGION

We are surrounded by phenomena which we are unable to understand. Whether we consider everyday experience, science, philosophy or religion, we shall always be forced to return to Pascal's dictum that 'there is an infinity of things which are beyond reason'.* There is the problem of birth with which the Existentialists are much pre-occupied—why am I born into this particular age, into a country and family which I could not choose, with a character and faculties which I must accept; there is the problem of death—why am I born to die? These and many other facts—that we live in a universe whose nature remains veiled to us, and on one of the tiniest bodies in it, that we do not know why there is matter, why there is life—such facts as these make it impossible, as we have said, to answer the question 'Why?' in any fundamental context. Yet it is exactly these inexplicable phenomena which form the basis and framework of our lives. We have to come to terms with them, and if our existence is to have a meaning they must, in one way or the other, make sense.

All these phenomena can be called irrational. This means, according to the Oxford Dictionary, 'unreasonable, illogical, absurd'; something which defies the intellect, which cannot be grasped by reason in a fully satisfactory way. It can be equated with senseless. But 'irrational' can also be interpreted as having another meaning, namely 'supra-rational'—some-

* See p. 8.

thing which remains an insoluble problem, a mystery, but which nevertheless indicates a hidden, higher meaning, something transcending reason which can yet be seen as meaningful. Existentialism could be described as being placed between these two poles of the irrational; while the absolute Existentialists emphasize the irrational as a challenge which should lead to the disclosure of a deeper meaning, but are forced, in the end, to embrace senselessness, others, like Kierkegaard, Jaspers and Buber, and like Pascal in an earlier age, discover meaning in that sphere which transcends reason.

As these inexplicable phenomena are the most basic ones, the question as to which of the two meanings the word 'irrational' has—absurd or supra-rational—can help us judge the relevance of any human endeavour in the effort to give sense to our existence. In particular, it can help the philosopher to evaluate the two disciplines which are outside philosophy and yet bound to figure largely in any philosophical discussion, as they have done in ours—that is, science and religion.

Before entering upon a further discussion of science, however, I should like to forestall a possible misunderstanding. We had to point out the limitations of science, and we shall have to do so again, in the sense that we must ensure that it is not applied outside its proper sphere. This does not mean that the philosophy expounded here is in any way anti-scientific, though Existentialism often is. Nor does our usage of 'the scientist' imply that no scientist is ever aware of these limitations; many of them are, while many non-scientists are not. The philosopher is concerned with an attitude, a special discipline, not with passing judgment on individual men. But today, with science triumphant, it is one of his most important tasks to reject any fallacious claims made by science. This, after all, is important for science itself, too, for dogmatic statements can hinder the progress of science, which is based on a continually changing set of theories. Actually, by making metaphysical speculations about nature superfluous, science has freed philosophy from a great burden, but it is altogether wrong for scientists or non-scientists now, in their turn, to try to make science an all-inclusive metaphysical explanation of existence, or to suggest that it is the only way of understanding anything at all fully. It is only with this fallacious philosophical extension of science that we are concerned.

Such fallacious claims are frequently due to the overlooking of a basic fact—that modern science has made an end of the rational attitude of the Middle Ages and become fundamentally irrational. Scholasticism had tried to find an all-inclusive rational explanation of the whole of existence; there was God as the First Cause of everything that ever happened, as Prime Mover, originating motion, as Creator; since the concept 'God' was then completely accepted as denoting something undoubtedly real, these explanations seemed to stand the test of reason. Modern scientific method was defined at its beginning by Francis Bacon, when he said: 'In physics they (the final causes) are impertinent . . . and hinder the sciences from holding their course of improvement',[1] and when he replaced deduction by induction. Deduction, an 'inference from general to particular', is a purely logical operation, while induction, the 'inferring of general law from particular instances',[2] is much less rational than Bacon himself thought, because we cannot be aware of all the instances which occur and must therefore generalize with the possibility of the existence of exceptions. But induction has become the modern scientific method. A further important step in its development was Galileo's rejection of all speculation about the origin of movement; science should be concerned solely with the observation of existing movements. As a result, science rests on the acceptance of 'brute facts', on their observation, their weighing, measuring, testing, without further questions being asked. There is no explanation why these facts are given; this irrational basis is simply taken for granted, and reason is employed only thereafter.

We have, in the first and second chapters, mentioned several examples of science going beyond reason—the quantum theory, the theory of evolution, theories about the origin of the universe.* In all these cases we discerned elements which defy reason, which are really *unthinkable*. The basic fact which has to be accepted in all these theories is the occurrence of some kind of inexplicable irregularity which gives rise to change and development. The development which leads to the order of the universe we know, in short, is brought about by disorder, with the help of accidents and blind forces, while reason demands that order should result from an attempt to create order on the basis of guiding principles.

To return once more to one of the examples—we have referred to two theories about the origin of the universe, to the theory that matter was originally extremely concentrated, and to the other according to which matter was thinly spread throughout the whole of space.† In both cases some irregularity which cannot be understood had to start the process of creating the universe. There is also a third theory, that of 'continuous creation', the belief, that is, that matter is continuously created out of nothing. Professor Fred Hoyle, who holds this theory, emphasizes very strongly that it really is a creation of atoms out of nothing: 'From time to time people ask where the created material comes from. Well it does not come from anywhere. Material simply appears—it is created. At one time the various atoms composing the material do not exist and at a later time they do.'[1] This contradicts another well-established philosophical claim: that something cannot be

* See esp. pp. 2–3, 20–3.   † See pp. 21–2.

created from nothing. This again is, in fact, *unthinkable*; if nothing could create something, it would have certain creative faculties and thus no longer be nothing.

Wherever we look in science, we shall discover such irrationality. In the theory of relativity, to give a last example, time and distance have become 'relative', that is, their length is no longer constant, but dependent on other factors. Yet the theory is based on the assumption that the speed of light is absolutely constant, even though there is no longer any way to ascertain such constancy, nor to establish absoluteness. As Nicolai Hartmann says: 'What should we think of a constancy of the speed of light which is supposed to exist in that space and time which have become relative? Constancy of speed means that during equal periods equal distances are continuously traversed. What, however, are "equal" periods and "equal" distances if time and space can expand and shrink? The conclusion which points towards the absolute constancy of speed of light meets the inevitable difficulty that its result abolishes the presuppositions of the possibility of constancy and inconstancy. The theory abolishes its own presuppositions.'[1] A fact which defies reason has simply to be accepted.

The way in which science includes the irrational is therefore, from the point of view of human experience, utterly unsatisfactory, and this makes it even more imperative to recognize its limitations. If this is not done, the irrational element in science represents a grave danger. Science—not only in physics, but increasingly in biology and physiology—has come more and more to penetrate and affect the basic structure of the physical universe; even the warnings of Bacon and Galileo are no longer heeded, as the theories about the origin of the universe show. But the irrational remains senseless; the essential foundations of human existence are invaded and made absurd. We are enabled to dominate nature, but become the prey—unless there is a counterweight to science—to unthinkable statements and inhuman numbers and thus become strangers to ourselves; inner experiences, values, morality, responsibility are undermined because the irrational, as dealt with by science, loses all value and meaning. How far the danger has already gone is shown by the fact that absurdity has become a value in itself both in absolute Existentialism (which, though opposed to science, mirrors our present situation clearly) and in art (which should, above all, help us to experience meaning).

We must therefore remain aware of the fact that scientific knowledge is not the truth by which we can live. The irrational cannot be avoided; if we are to live a meaningful life, however, the irrational must become supra-rational, an indication of the transcendental. We are unable to seize the whole truth; any knowledge we may achieve is limited; we only grasp facets of truth. Yet fundamentally truth is one, and each of its facets reflects its nature. If science is not recognized as a completely different kind of knowledge, but accepted as a facet of truth, this facet will force upon us conclusions regarding the whole truth, and thus the whole truth, including that by which we live, will be in danger of becoming impersonal and of being robbed of its value. We shall return to this point after discussing other aspects of the irrational.

Nor does religion solve the problems of existence; it does not give complete rational explanations; but it causes inner experiences which give meaning to the irrational. This process is neither absurd nor 'mystical' nor difficult to understand; it can be appreciated in the context of everyday experience, as a few examples taken from outside the sphere of religion may show.

There is, for instance, the problem of space and time,

which we have just mentioned as a stumbling block in the theory of relativity. These two concepts can be neither fully explained nor explained away, and we certainly cannot say why space and time exist. But they can make sense when they are seen in an 'existential' way.

In external reality, both concepts are purely formal and entirely abstract, so that they can be measured and expressed by numbers. These measurements become something real in our lives, too; we are spatial bodies, living at a certain place, and we have to cross distances; periods of time are made real by day and night, by the calendar, by seasons and feasts, by growing older. Yet this does not exhaust the significance of space and time for us.

The experience of time—to take it first because it is more intimately connected with inner experience—makes this strikingly clear. If we experience something very interesting or important, time passes quickly and we hardly notice the passing of hours or even days; but if we are bored, or doing routine work or work we do not like, time seems to move very slowly indeed; a few minutes may appear like hours and no day ever seems to end. This impression, however, is completely reversed in retrospect; for those apparently endless periods in which we had no satisfactory experience shrink or even disappear in our memory, while a few hours or days which were of importance to us or full of events appear much longer than they actually were. The experience of time, therefore, does not depend upon its measurable length alone.

This is equally true of our lives. We live so and so many years, but this does not tell the whole story; we can make proper use of our time and thus live our lives fully and enrich them, or waste our time and lose it. Time is not a simple possession; it has to be conquered. This makes the experience of time a constant urge, similar to conscience; we feel that we ought to make the right use of time, so that we do not lose it. The urge is not identical with conscience, for it can be satisfied not only by moral but also by very different actions or impressions—by strong sensual experiences, for instance, or by adventures, by interesting activities or by the impact of beauty. But it is probably even stronger and more constant than conscience. Therefore, if we are unable to make proper use of time, we want to 'kill' it in order to get rid of its constant challenge, to forget that it is passing beyond retrieve. Once the challenge is not satisfied time becomes an enemy and we have to fight against it. It is very difficult to bear a long period of boredom with equanimity, at least without deadening one's feelings to an undesirable degree. Yet the challenge is never completely silenced by the mere killing of time, nor by indulging in senseless industry to which it may also lead; there remains an ever-present knowledge of waste. Full satisfaction can only be achieved if we succeed in giving to time the right content.

Space, as an actual experience, also represents a challenge— the urge to do something in opposition to the fact that we are so infinitesimally small when compared with the space which surrounds us. The ideal of the great hero who, like Alexander or Napoleon, sets out to increase his own size by conquering space, by subjugating people and by thus adding their strength and land to his own stature, has always been one of the most powerful ideals, for both the heroes and the hero-worshippers, because to conquer and acquire space directly seems to be the simplest reaction to the overwhelming size of even the earth. The same urge is probably also at work in those technical developments which try to overcome space by greater and greater speed. But all these attempts are obviously futile; even if a man conquered the whole earth, even when, as now, he is able to reach its farthest points in an astonishingly short time, he still must remain infinitesimally small when compared with the universe, and this situation is hardly rectified even by an invasion of outer space.

The challenge of space requires a different answer. We cannot possibly hope to become equal to space in spatial terms, but we can hope to find our right place in the universe. If a man fulfils his right task, if he does something which he believes is of unchallengeable importance, he can achieve a harmony in which his inner certainty makes his external smallness insignificant. The challenge of space seems to be less consciously felt today than that of time, but it is still felt and should be made conscious, for it provides us with an essential criterion for our actions. The experience of space is so overwhelming that, when we scrutinize our endeavours in its light, we are really made aware of whether or not our endeavours are of the right kind. How can we ever hope to withstand the apparently annihilating extension of space? Thus, while time urges us to embark on activities which are important, space points more directly to where this importance is to be found—in actions and experiences which are truly significant. Space, in fact, leads on to the absolute values.

The challenge of space and time is most beautifully expressed by Kant in a famous statement of which usually only a single sentence is quoted. I should like to quote it here more fully, to bring out the point which is of importance to us—the need to give meaning to the irrational. This statement, too, can be understood with the help of everyday experience, but to understand it is also to understand how religious experiences work. Kant says:

'Two things fill the mind with ever new and increasing admiration and awe, the oftener and more steadily we reflect on them: the starry heavens above and the moral law within. I have not to search for them and conjecture them as though they were veiled in darkness or were in the transcendent region beyond my horizon; I see them before me and connect them directly with the consciousness of my existence. The former begins from the place which I occupy in the external world of sense, and enlarges my connexion therein to an unbounded extent with worlds upon worlds and systems of systems, and moreover into limitless times of their periodic motion, its beginning and continuance. The second begins from my invisible self, my personality, and exhibits me in a world which has true infinity, but which is traceable only by the understanding . . . The former view of a countless multitude of worlds annihilates as it were my importance as an animal creature, which after it has been for a short time provided with vital power, one knows not how, must again give back the matter of which it was formed to the planet it inhabits (a mere speck in the universe). The second on the contrary infinitely elevates my worth as an intelligence by my personality, in which the moral law reveals to me a life independent of animality and even of the whole sensible world.'[1]

There is, in this, a contradiction which cannot be resolved. All explanations which try to bridge the gap between man's external insignificance and his inner significance have broken down and will break down, for all of them are bound to overemphasize one of the two sides. But if we accept the contradiction as such and think both these contradictory thoughts simultaneously, as an 'absolute paradox', we shall have an experience of the majesty of the universe and of both the wretchedness and greatness of man which will be clearer and more meaningful than any rational explanation. It will give reality to that supra-rational sphere which goes beyond what can be expressed directly by words.

That the contradiction has to be accepted can also be seen

when we consider our reactions to space and time together. Time leads to death, so that we are certainly destroyed so far as we exist in space and time. But there is something in us which cannot be crushed by the size of space, because it has no relation to size; this 'something' becomes tangible in the 'moral law within' which is also more permanent than the single individual. Can our death in space and time then really destroy us? The moral law points, as Kant says, to a 'true infinity' which transcends both the endlessness of space and that of time.

All this means that space and time, purely abstract and formal in external reality, are *not neutral* when actually experienced. They demand that we should live in the face of *truth*, accept responsibility, do something of real value, especially *the good*, but they also point to the third of the traditional absolute values, for the impact of *beauty* can also enable us to face space and time by an experience of the transcendental. All these experiences remain irrational, because they involve contradictions which cannot be solved rationally, but as we meet the irrational in the way which space and time indicate, it makes sense. It gives us access to the foundation of all reality.

My second example is another of those age-old philosophical problems which have defied solution throughout the centuries—that of necessity and freedom. We have discussed it several times,* but I should like now to bring together the different threads of thought which we have touched. Once more, we are confronted by the irrational, but we can give it meaning.

In external reality, as grasped by natural science, necessity is dominant. There are gaps, accidents, contingencies, but the scientist tries to fill these gaps; the fewer gaps left, the better his grasp. Since his method is designed to discover necessity

* See esp. pp. 5–6, 13–14, 93–5, 122–3.

he can never account for freedom; the farthest he can get in this direction is his description of the indeterminacy of the behaviour of electrons. This still cannot account for human freedom, which is not merely indeterminacy but a conscious direction of choices, decisions and actions. The so-called freedom of the electron is really a misnomer, for although we cannot predict its next move, this move will be determined by factors which are not the electron's choice. Certainly, psychologists show that our actions, too, are often determined by factors over which we had no influence, but we have seen that this is not the whole truth.

Yet even though freedom cannot be discovered with the help of the objective method, it is nevertheless correct to make it the basis of the subjective method, for we shall never be able to understand man unless we assume his freedom from the start. Nobody—not even I myself if I believe in determinism—will finally convince me that I lack freedom completely, that I cannot, for instance, lift my arm when I want to lift it. This example may sound trivial, but it is really fundamental, for it applies to all my decisions, including my moral ones. I may often be mistaken and think myself free when I am actually succumbing to external or internal compulsions, but such mistakes do not invalidate the fundamental fact that I am free to decide, that I can become aware of such compulsions and take them into account when coming to decisions. Otherwise I should have to discard all feeling of responsibility.

The subjective method enables us to distinguish between two forms of freedom which we have called *freedom of choice* and *choice of freedom*.* Obviously, a free choice must precede any free decision or action, but we have said that we can make a wrong choice—money, success in a career, any kind

---

* See pp. 122–3.

of fanaticism—which enslaves us again. The error of the absolute Existentialists was that they only acknowledged the freedom of choice and did not see that freedom must find expression in actions which agree with the true nature of man; they did not want to accept that the fact that we are human beings indicates the direction in which freedom should be exercised. Freedom can be defined as acting in complete agreement with our true nature, without the influence of compulsion foreign to it. This, however, raises the question which the extreme Existentialists neglected—what is man's true nature?

Our investigation has probably made clear by now that man really is a citizen of two worlds—that he is a product of biological evolution and thus possesses what could be called an animal nature, and that he is invaded by the transcendental and therefore also possesses what can perhaps best be called a spiritual nature. It is this duality which makes it necessary to use both the objective and the subjective method which, in their turn, give greater concreteness to these two aspects of man's being.

Both his animal and his spiritual nature could be regarded in much the same way. Man finds great satisfaction if he succeeds in giving full expression to either of the two; we admire both the man of great vitality and the saint. Both natures have also to be restricted in practical life; to give full expression to all animal instincts would soon prove destructive, and the purely practical tasks of everyday life would hardly be properly fulfilled if we only did justice to spiritual demands. Man has to become a social being; on the one hand, he must not give free rein to all his physical desires and his selfishness; on the other he must at times be prepared to accept, at least within the limits we have discussed,* means against which moral

* See pp. 76–7.

objections could be raised, and he must be able to choose, if necessary, the lesser of two evils. Any all-inclusive absoluteness, as we have seen, falsifies knowledge, and it also makes us overlook the limitations imposed upon man by the conditions of his existence.

There are, nevertheless, obvious differences between these two aspects of man's nature—differences which help us to come to a decision about his 'true' nature. His desire for some kind of absoluteness is justified; we have said that the absolute knowledge of his being in existence challenges him to find an absolute answer to the question of the meaning of this unexplained fact.* But as this answer cannot be in the form of a generalized and all-embracing statement, it must be sought in a specific direction.

Even this limited absoluteness, however, cannot be found when we look in the direction of animality, for any complete and unfettered giving in to it would undoubtedly debase man. We admire great vitality, the great conqueror, even the great criminal, but the admiration cannot be made absolute because it obliges us to ignore all the harm done, the killing, murder. Even Nietzsche's superman, the greatest and most consistent attempt to base an ideal on man's animal nature, only helps us to see that it must fail. But complete harmony and ultimate satisfaction can be found in those experiences which give greater reality to man's spiritual nature, and here absoluteness can be admitted without restriction; harmony and satisfaction will be greatest when that nature can make itself fully felt, transcending all practical demands. We need only think of Kierkegaard's 'leap into the unknown' or of the *I-Thou* relationship to see that this claim is justified.

In most of these experiences there is one element which can easily be discerned—morality. Is there any objection to

* See p. 139.

accepting Kierkegaard's 'ethical self' as a description of man's true nature? On the one hand, ethics still keeps within the boundaries of philosophy, as our discussion of freedom demands; morality is that aspect of religion which can be philosophically discussed. On the other hand, no restrictions are required when man gives expression to this side of his nature; choices based on the ethical self thus fulfil the demands of what we have called the choice of freedom; they will not enslave man again. It is true that too narrow an interpretation of morality could enslave man, too; but Kierkegaard has shown that the ethical self must be understood as the result of a breaking into man's existence of the transcendental, for otherwise love could not be commanded.* This brings in the fullness of man's spiritual nature, and this will set us free—free to love.

Another objection could perhaps still be raised—that this is a circular argument: freedom is defined as demanding guidance by the true nature of man, and this nature is then defined according to the demands of freedom. But once we reach the very foundations of existence, this kind of argument is inevitable and legitimate; as no further step is possible, basic elements can only point to each other. That no other argument is feasible even confirms that we have reached the foundations.

This is, once more, confirmed by our actual experience. The realm of freedom cannot be theoretically circumscribed; we cannot say that so far we are free and that there our freedom ends. We must proceed by trial and error, so as to find out what has to be accepted and what can be changed; we must constantly test the boundaries of freedom. The best starting point to do so will be to accept the ethical self as our true nature and to act according to it; if we begin in this way,

---

* See p. 67–8.

the interaction between freedom and the 'true' self will gradually clarify both. Each correct decision will help us to recognize our nature better; it will show us the regions where we can really act in obedience solely to ourselves; we shall feel that we are set free. Thereby we shall be led to acquire a greater certainty in arriving at correct decisions and these, in their turn, will give us a more reliable knowledge of our true self. Gradually, the sphere of our inner experiences will widen, will bring in the religious implications of morality, and will thus give a fuller meaning to the term 'spiritual reality'.

We have to admit that the problem of necessity and freedom, too, cannot be solved rationally. In external reality both concepts remain purely formal, necessity meaning that all effects are determined by their causes, even those effects whose causes we do not, or do not as yet, know, but human freedom would mean that man's will can be a new, first cause of an action not otherwise determined. Such a first cause cannot be accounted for in the world of natural laws, for these do not allow exceptions; it cannot even be accommodated within the realm of probability which has led to some uncertainty about necessity. The acceptance of human freedom remains irrational. But once again these two concepts, when actually experienced, are *not neutral*. Both are, like space and time, very real as inner experiences; necessity, as external and internal compulsion, showing us our place in the universe which cannot be changed, and freedom giving access to the richness and fullness of human nature and showing us that, in the face of the most overwhelming challenges, it can yet assert itself. The contradiction between these two concepts, even though insoluble, can guide our actions, and if it does, the irrational will again make sense, pointing towards that supra-rational reality which gives content to religion.

More examples leading to the same conclusions could

easily be given. There is, for instance, the third of the old fundamental problems of philosophy—that of the One and the Many. But we need not add much to what has already been said.

These two concepts are of the utmost importance to our grasp of external reality, for they form the basis of numbers and mathematics. But there they, too, remain abstract, and we cannot answer the question why external reality appears to us in such a way that we need them. We are always trying to grasp the oneness of existence and always failing to do so because the barrier of the Many—the fact that there are many things or many men, for instance—proves both insuperable and inexplicable.

Numbers do not apply to inner experiences. If I feel pain and someone else begins to feel pain, it cannot be said that the quantity of pain has now doubled; feelings cannot be related to each other as mere quantities. Nor do numbers apply in the moral sphere; the one Socrates was right against a vast majority; the quantitative relationship—that a majority should have greater weight than a single individual—had no significance in matters of right and wrong, even though it was very important in its practical effect. Nevertheless, the One and the Many become real to us in inner experience, for we are single individuals among many, men among men. The experiences which thus arise have been explored in our discussion of the *I–Thou* relationship. Even this relationship, however, does not solve the problem which these two concepts represent; we do not know why there are many single individuals, different persons meeting on a common ground; why there is the *I*, the *Thou*, and in addition the *It*, and why none of these can ever be omitted. Yet once more the two concepts are reliable guides to the giving of meaning to our existence. The One and the Many, too, are *not neutral;* if we follow the direction they indicate, our experience will lead to the greatest possible satisfaction, and the meeting with the human *Thou* will enable us to experience the final *Thou*. We shall live face to face with God.

These examples taken from the realm of philosophy have probably shown, too, how it is that religion transforms the irrational into a meaningful experience. Most religions use a large number of contradictions which, looked at from outside, seem irrational in a meaningless way, but, when experienced, help to make accessible what otherwise could not be expressed in language at all. Our thoughts are driven, in opposite directions, to the utmost boundaries they can reach; but the absolute paradox, once experienced, makes sense.

In Christianity there is, for instance, judgment and grace. They form a complete contradiction, but mere logical thought is driven towards both. If each single individual is important, as Christian teaching claims, his deeds must be of real consequence, so that they have to be judged, even in the last reckoning. On the other hand, the grace of God cannot possibly be limited; any kind of limitation or restriction cannot be reconciled with the Christian conception of God, least of all a restriction caused by our human actions. Nevertheless, in spite of their contradiction, we have to think of both judgment and grace at the same time; for if we stress judgment alone, God will no longer remain the God of Love, and if we stress grace alone, how can it matter what we do or whether we try to become worthy of this love? We shall be tempted to remain idle. If, however, we accept the contradiction, our feelings will gradually disclose to us a new harmony. If we are in despair about our sinfulness and weighed down by our sins, the knowledge that the judgment rests not with us but with God can be experienced as redeeming grace; if we are hardened and unaware of our sins, a sudden insight into what grace really means can reveal our sins to us in their full significance, so that grace is experienced as severe punishment. Yet this 'fear and trembling' leads to faith, and it is thus that we are no longer in danger of reducing our experiences or the conception of God to mere abstract notions.

The problem of predestination and free will is similar. Again, logical thought must, on the basis of Christianity, come to both conclusions—that our lives are predestined and, at the same time, that we are free and responsible for what we are doing. If God is all-knowing, our destinies must be known to Him from the beginning and cannot be changed by us. But, if our lives are to be of any consequence, they cannot be completely determined, not even by a necessity based on the will of God. Religion, after all, is meant to set us free. An explanation which leans to one side or the other is bound to lead to a falsification of Christian faith; emphasis on predestination alone will rob our actions of any significance and make us mere puppets in the hands of God; emphasis on freedom alone will lead to that kind of liberalism which robs Christian religion of all its particular characteristics. But if we accept the contradiction and try to live it, the absolute paradox will make us experience what we have tried to describe when discussing Kant's 'starry heavens above' and 'the moral law within'.

I hope that it has become clear by now that the irrational can acquire a supra-rational meaning. Instead of dwelling further on this point, I should therefore prefer, in conclusion, to raise a different question—what can the philosopher do to prevent the irrational from invading our lives in a meaningless and destructive way, what can he do to ensure that it is approached in a manner which contributes to the enrichment of our lives in such a way as to give meaning to them? Our discussion has shown that this can be done, but there is no doubt that only few are aware of it, that the attempt to do so remains, in our present situation, very nearly powerless. What can the philosopher do to support this attempt and make it influence our lives?

We are, at the present moment, confronted with a paradox, very different from those we have discussed so far. On the one hand, no power in the world seems able to stop the progress of science, nor does this seem desirable; on the other hand, we can by now imagine a situation in which the progress of science might have to be controlled, a situation in which man ought to have the strength to renounce the use of some of those dangerous new discoveries which threaten human existence. Confronted with this situation, the power of the philosopher is certainly extremely small, but many of our examples have shown that his position is not altogether hopeless; books can have unpredictable consequences, they can exercise power. To prove the importance of his endeavours, the philosopher should deal with this all-important paradox.

A prerequisite of any possible change is to see the problem clearly, and this task falls within the province of philosophy. It has become a commonplace to say that one of our difficulties consists in the fact that our moral development lags so far behind our scientific development, and this, commonplace or not, is undoubtedly correct. But it is hardly sufficient to make such a statement and leave it at that. To make clearer what it implies we have to reject another commonplace. It is equally often said that science is neutral, that it is not the task of the scientist to decide what use is made of his discoveries, but that of the politician, of society, of all of us. This claim, however, does not do justice to experience. The human mind has only a limited power; to disregard limitations is, here too, a fallacy; if some of man's mental faculties are enormously developed, as the rational ones have been for a long time, perhaps for centuries, other mental faculties will be weakened and the human mind impoverished. In other words, science is also *not neutral*; too great concentration on it undermines the development of exactly those forces which would be needed to ensure the right use of science.

The answer to this problem which we have tried to give in this book is to advocate the application of both the objective and the subjective method, which means, under the present circumstances, seeing the limitations of the objective method and developing the subjective method more fully. The development of European thought has gone, in the main, from extreme to extreme; the Middle Ages concentrated so exclusively on spiritual problems that, as a reaction, over-concentration on external, material reality became inevitable. There have been minor deviations, of course, ever since the Middle Ages, but they have hardly had any influence on this movement from the one extreme to the other. We are still dominated by the second extreme, but there are signs that there could be a reaction, leading again to another extreme. One should never forget that catastrophes, or even disenchantment or apathy, can make apparently improbable developments possible. The absolute Existentialists embrace nothingness, despair, the absurd; they accept the meaningless irrational as an end in itself; and absurdity has proved attractive in many spheres of modern life. Any such violent reaction against science, however, would obviously be wrong, as some manifestations of Existentialism show; our task should be to create a balance, a proper relationship between the two extremes which are both necessary for a full life. The objective and the subjective methods do justice to both; their correct application, therefore, could create a balance.

To give proper weight to the subjective method (which is appreciated only by a tiny minority today), philosophers should support a provocative step which has been made by some Existentialists, though it has perhaps not yet attracted enough attention. They should insist that the word 'truth' must not be used for scientific statements, but only for that truth by which we live, the truth disclosed by the subjective method.

We have said before that we must acknowledge two different kinds of truth, and used as an illustration an encyclopaedia which, though containing a large number of correct statements, will hardly be considered as a repository of that truth by which we live.* We have also mentioned that truth, though we can only grasp some of its facets, is fundamentally one, and that, if impersonal scientific statements are accepted as truth, the whole truth will therefore be distorted.† For this reason it would probably be better not to talk about two kinds of truth, but to restrict the use of the word to the realm of personal experience.

Until very recently, truth was simply regarded as one of the absolute values. This claim has lost much of its meaning for us; when thinking of truth we probably think first of correct scientific statements, and hardly understand why truth should be called a value. Yet in important, personal experiences we certainly still seek, or meet, a truth which can only be described as an absolute value. The claim that truth is a value means that we have to see it as valuable for us; it requires our judgment; and to make this judgment absolutely reliable, truth has to influence our lives; it requires personal participation; it must be acted upon. It cannot be proved, but 'must shine in its own light';¹ it must appeal to our sense of truth so strongly that to deny it would completely contradict all our experience and appear nonsensical in the light of what we, in fact, experience as truth. If we are

* See p. 101.   † See p. 166.

honest, we cannot but accept it; we would deeply hurt ourselves if we acted against it; it would be like banging our
head against a wall. Our investigation has shown us a large
number of such truths, or facets of truth, especially in the
fourth, fifth and eighth chapters. Such commandments as
that we should love our neighbour, or that we must not kill,
and such experiences as the *I–Thou* relationship, obviously
require to be accepted as truth. Naturally, as truth cannot be
proved, it has constantly to be tested by experience, and this
should—in contrast to the common attitude today which
insists on tests in science, but takes important facets of truth
half-unconsciously for granted—become one of the main
preoccupations of both the philosophers and of every one of
us. For as we cannot live without accepting, consciously or
unconsciously, some kind of truth, we should strive to know
by which truth we live.

I have dealt with the problem of truth elsewhere, and I do
not wish to repeat myself.[1] But I hope that I have said enough
to show that this change in the usage of the word 'truth'
could help to throw into relief the importance of the subjective method and that this, though it may still appear to some
a small contribution in terms of practical life, could help
considerably to create that balance between science and morality which we lack. This would represent a major achievement
in any terms. The scientists could hardly object to it; there is
at present a discrepancy between the support different branches
of science receive; greater balance in general could produce
greater balance in the realm of science. If one sees the need
for both the objective and the subjective methods, the emphasis
on the subjective method, even though it is what is most
needed today, is never anti-scientific. On the other hand, to
insist that truth can be found by the subjective method alone,
could help to improve this method, too. Experience has to

be admitted as evidence; but is it always tested carefully enough? If personal experience is seen as the only way to truth, testing in this sphere will become—in its different way—as exacting as it is in science, and thus the importance and reliability of the subjective method will be more easily recognized. It could then lead beyond Existentialism towards a more balanced philosophy.

In fact, we have moved beyond Existentialism already. Not only have the wrong claims of absolute Existentialism been left far behind; if our treatment of the irrational is correct, we are led even beyond Kierkegaard's austerity, beyond his overemphasis on 'fear and trembling', to an act of faith which, even if necessarily transcending reason, can be supported by reason. It is true that Kierkegaard uses the dread instilled by the absurd to make accessible the meaningfulness of religion; but his stressing of absurdity has made a deeper impression on most modern Existentialists than his Christianity, and thus a desperate struggle against the senselessness of the irrational has become a characteristic of their philosophy. Even many of the less extreme Existentialists, who could not be called 'absolute', pay too exclusive attention to destructive experiences.* Such philosophers as Buber are rare exceptions. However, in this chapter we have shown that the irrational, in both philosophy and religion, need not be seen as absurd, but can make sense and give meaning directly to the transcendental. On this basis, all those elements in Existentialism which we found necessary and valuable could be included in philosophy, which could once again justify its claim to be one of the most important endeavours of the human mind.

* This kind of Existentialism we have not discussed, but our short reference to Jaspers can serve as an illustration. See pp. 137–8.

REFERENCES

PAGE 2

1. *Philosophic Problems of Nuclear Science*, London 1952, p. 93.

PAGE 8

1. *Pensées*, No. 267 (Everyman Library).

PAGE 15

1. *The Rebel* (New York, 1954), p. 5.
2. *Ibid.* p. 209.

PAGE 21

1. *Essays of a Biologist*, p. 176.

PAGE 24

1. *Die fröhliche Wissenschaft*, § 349. This remark is perhaps not wholly unjustified in view of Malthus's strong influence upon Darwin.
2. *The Complete Works*, ed. by Dr Oscar Levy, Vol. 7, *Human, All Too Human*, p. 43. (When I have used existing English translations, I refer to them by their English titles; where I have made my own translation, the German titles are given.)

PAGE 25

1. *Menschliches, Allzumenschliches*, I, § 501.
2. *Ibid.* § 44.
3. *Ibid.* § 50.
4. *Ibid.* § 74.
5. *The Complete Works*, Vol. 7, *Human All Too Human*, p. 211.
6. *Ibid.* p. 71.
7. *Ibid.* p. 127.

PAGE 27

1. *The Complete Works*, Vol. 10, *The Joyful Wisdom*, p. 294.
2. *The Complete Works*, Vol. 5, *Beyond Good and Evil*, p. 117.

PAGE 28

1. *Menschliches Allzumenschliches*, I, § 114.
2. *The Complete Works*, Vol. 7, *Human, All Too Human*, p. 43.
3. *Menschliches Allzumenschliches*, I, § 110.
4. *The Complete Works*, Vol. 5, *Beyond Good and Evil*, p. 189.
5. *Menschliches Allzumenschliches*, I, § 241.
6. *Beyond Good and Evil*, p. 224.
7. *Die fröhliche Wissenschaft*, § 92.

PAGE 29

1. *Menschliches Allzumenschliches*, I, § 477.
2. *Götzendämmerung*, 'Moral als Widernatur', § 3.
3. *Zur Genealogie der Moral*, I. Abh., § 11.
4. *The Complete Works*, Vol. 15, *The Will to Power*, p. 20.

PAGE 30

1. *The Complete Works*, Vol. 10, *The Joyful Wisdom*, p. 164.
2. *Der Wille zur Macht*, § 634. (Kröner Edition).

PAGE 31

1. *The Complete Works*, Vol. 15, *The Will to Power*, p. 432.

PAGE 32

1. *The Possessed*, Everyman's Library, II, pp. 254–55.
2. *Also sprach Zarathustra*, II, ch. 2.

PAGE 33

1. *Jenseits von Gut und Böse*, § 199, and *Die fröhliche Wissenschaft* § 362.

PAGE 35

1. *Jenseits von Gut und Böse*, § 264.
2. *The Complete Works*, Vol. 16, *The Twilight of the Idols*, p. 47, and *Menschliches Allzumenschliches*, II., § 278.

PAGE 36

1. *The Listener*, Vol. XLVI., pp. 878–9. (Italics mine.)

PAGE 37

1. *Ibid.*

References

PAGE 38
1. *Der Fall Wagner*, § 11.
2. Letters to his sister, 20th May, 1885 and 26th December, 1887.

PAGE 40
1. *Die fröhliche Wissenschaft*, § 125.

PAGE 41
1. *Ibid.* § 125.

PAGE 43
1. *Der Wille zur Macht*, § 693.
2. *Ibid.* § 30.
3. *Ibid.* §§ 23, 24.
4. *Ibid.* § 36.

PAGE 44
1. *Ibid.* § 38.
2. *Ibid.* § 39.

PAGE 45
1. *Ibid.* § 75.
2. *The Complete Works*, Vol. 15, *The Will to Power*, p. 104.

PAGE 46
1. *Der Wille zur Macht*, § 32.
2. *Ibid.* § 29.
3. *Ibid.* § 34.

PAGE 49
1. *Pensées*, Nos. 205–6.

PAGE 50
1. Letter to Freiherr von Gersdorff, 20th October, 1870.
2. *Nietzsche contra Wagner*. Wie ich von Wagner loskam. § 2.
3. *Die fröhliche Wissenschaft*, § 124, and *Menschliches Allzumensch-liches*, I., § 248.

PAGE 51
1. *Die fröhliche Wissenschaft*, Vorrede zur 2. Ausgabe, § 3.
2. *Ibid.* § 285.

PAGE 52

1. *The Complete Works, Vol. 15, The Will to Power*, p. 432.
2. *Der Wille zur Macht*, § 226.
3. *Ibid.* § 229.

PAGE 54

1. *Götzendämmerung*, 'Die Vernunft in der Philosophie', § 2.

PAGE 57

1. *Repetition*, Oxford 1942, p. 112.
2. *Ibid.* p. 114.
3. *Pensées*, No. 205.

PAGE 58

1. *Repetition*, p. 125.
2. *Fear and Trembling*, Princeton 1941, p. 44.
3. *Ibid.* p. 21.

PAGE 59

1. *Ibid.* p. 24.

PAGE 60

1. *Ibid.* p. 187.

PAGE 61

1. *Ibid.* p. 78.

PAGE 62

1. *Ibid.* p. 79.

PAGE 63

1. All three passages in *Fear and Trembling*, pp. 151–2.

PAGE 68

1. *Works of Love*, Princeton 1946, p. 289.
2. *Ibid.* p. 262.
3. *Ibid.* p. 48.

References

PAGE 69

1. *Pensées*, Nos. 280 and 277.
2. For a further elaboration of this problem see P. Roubiczek, *Thinking in Opposites*, ch. VI, and *Thinking Towards Religion*, ch. V.

PAGE 70

1. *The Brothers Karamazov*, Everyman, I, 331.
2. *Works of Love*, pp. 66, 50.

PAGE 71

1. *Ibid*. p. 58.
2. *Ibid*. pp. 72-3.

PAGE 76

1. *Metaphysik der Sitten*, 2. Abschnitt.

PAGE 85

1. *An Introduction to Ethics*, London 1955, pp. 122-3.
2. *History of Western Philosophy*, London 1946, p. 800.

PAGE 93

1. Cf., for example, *The World and God*, London 1935, pp. 70-2. I am partly following Farmer's thought in this concluding part of the chapter.

PAGE 96

1. *Murder in the Cathedral*, London 1935, p. 44.

PAGE 98

1. *Grace and Personality*, Cambridge 1931, p. 62.

PAGE 100

1. *Pensées*, Nos. 277, 275, 30, 282.

PAGE 102

1. *Concluding Unscientific Postscript*, Princeton 1944, p. 281.
2. *Ibid*. p. 116.

PAGE 103

1. *Ibid*. p, 116.
2. *The Journals*, Oxford 1938, p. 153.

PAGE 104

1. *Concluding Unscientific Postscript*, p. 371.

PAGE 107

1. *Ibid.* p. 176.
2. *Fear and Trembling*, p. 50.

PAGE 108

1. *The Journals*, p. 544.
2. *Concluding Unscientific Postscript*, p. 327.
3. *The Point of View*, Oxford 1939, p. 35.

PAGE 119

1. *L'expérience intérieure*, Paris 1943, p. 109. I am indebted for this and some of the following quotations to *Existentialism* by P. Foulquié, translated by Kathleen Raine, London 1948. I would also like to acknowledge a debt to this book for some of my remarks about French Existentialists.

PAGE 120

1. *L'être et le néant*, Paris 1943, pp. 393, 633.

PAGE 121

1. In *Action*, 12th and 27th December, 1944.

PAGE 123

1. For a further discussion of the problems of freedom see P. Roubiczek, *Thinking towards Religion*, pp. 173 ff. and *Thinking in Opposites*, pp. 195 ff.
2. Sartre, *L'être et le néant*, pp. 520–1.

PAGE 125

1. *La nausée*, Paris 1942, p. 170, and *L'âge de raison*, Paris 1945, p. 664.
2. *Was ist Metaphysik?* Frankfurt am Main, 1949, p. 32.
3. *Pyrrhus et Cinéas*, Paris 1943, p. 67.
4. *Being and Time*, London 1962, p. 251.
5. J. Locke, *An Essay Concerning Human Understanding*, Bk. IV, ch. IV, 3

References

PAGE 126

1. *L'être et le néant*, p. 225. Heidegger tries to avoid this conclusion, but his final definition of being is empty. See p. 132.
2. *Ibid.* p. 527.

PAGE 127

1. In *Action*, 27th December, 1944.

PAGE 132

1. *Einführung in die Metaphysik*, Tübingen 1953, p. 154.

PAGE 134

1. In his work *Being and Time*.

PAGE 141

1. *I and Thou*, Edinburgh 1937, p. 11.

PAGE 151

1. *Das Problem des Menschen*, Heidelberg 1948, pp. 159–60.

PAGE 153

1. *Eclipse of God*, London 1953, pp. 68–9.

PAGE 157

1. Compare Kierkegaard's 'repetition'; see p. 120.

PAGE 158

1. *Reason and Emotion*, London 1935, pp. 103–104.

PAGE 159

1. *Eclipse of God*, p. 103.
2. *Ibid.* p. 166.

PAGE 163

1. *The Dignity and Advancement of Learning*, Bk. III, ch. 4.
2. Both definitions from *The Concise Oxford Dictionary*.

PAGE 164

1. *The Nature of the Universe*, Oxford 1950, p. 105.

PAGE 165

1. *Philosophie der Natur*, Berlin 1950, pp. 246 ff.

PAGE 170

1. *Critique of Practical Reason and other works on the theory of ethics,* London 1889, p. 260.

PAGE 182

1. H. H. Farmer, *God and Men*, London 1948, p. 18.

PAGE 183

1. See *Thinking towards Religion*, ch. VII, and *Thinking in Opposites*, ch. IX.

SELECT BIBLIOGRAPHY

Works which are published in many editions are cited by titles only. For other works a place and date of publication are given.

I STANDARD WORKS

BUBER, MARTIN. *I and Thou.* Edinburgh, 1937.
  Eclipse of God. London, 1953.
  Between Man and Man. London, 1947.

HEIDEGGER, MARTIN. *Being and Time.* London, 1962.
  Existence and Being. London, 1949.
  An Introduction to Metaphysics. New Haven, 1959.

JASPERS, KARL. *The Perennial Scope of Philosophy.* London, 1950.
  Man in the Modern Age. London, 1951.
  Reason and Existence. London, 1956.

KIERKEGAARD, SØREN. *Fear and Trembling.*
  Repetition.
  Works of Love.
  Concluding Unscientific Postcript.
  The Concept of Dread.
  The Journals.

NIETZSCHE, FRIEDRICH. *The Joyful Wisdom.*
  Human All Too Human.
  Thus Spake Zarathustra.
  Beyond Good and Evil.
  Genealogy of Morals.
  The Will to Power.

SARTRE, JEAN-PAUL. *Being and Nothingness.* London, 1957.
  Nausea. London, 1962.
  Existentialism and Humanism. London, 1948.

II GUIDE FOR FURTHER READING

BARRETT, W. *Irrational Man*. London, 1961.

BERDYAEV, N. *The Destiny of Man*. London, 1937.
  Slavery and Freedom. London, 1943.
  The Realm of the Spirit and the Realm of Caesar. London, 1952.

BRETALL, R. *A Kierkegaard Anthology*. Princeton, 1946.

BROCK, W. *An Introduction to Contemporary German Philosophy*.
  Cambridge, 1935.

CAMUS, A. *The Rebel*. London, 1953.

COHEN, A. A. *Buber*. London, 1957.

DOSTOEVSKY, F. *Notes from Underground*.
  The Possessed.
  The Brothers Karamazov.

FARMER, H. H. *God and Men*. London, 1948.
  The World and God. London, 1935.

FOULQUIE, P. *Existentialism*. London, 1948.

GRENE, M. *Heidegger*. London, 1957.

GRIFFITH, G. O. *Makers of Modern Thought*. London, 1948.

GUARDINI, R. *Freedom, Grace and Destiny*. London, 1961.
  The End of the Modern World. London, 1957.

LILLIE, W. *An Introduction to Ethics*. London, 1955.

LOWRIE, W. *A Short Life of Kierkegaard*. London, 1943.

LUBAC, H. DE. *The Drama of Atheist Humanism*. London, 1949.

MACMURRAY, J. *Reason and Emotion*. London, 1935.
  The Self as Agent. London, 1957.
  Persons in Relation. London, 1961.

MARCEL G. *Being and Having*. Westminster, 1949.
  The Philosophy of Existence. London, 1948.

MURDOCH, I. *Sartre*. Cambridge, 1953.

OMAN, J. *Grace and Personality*. Cambridge, 1931.
  The Natural and the Supernatural. Cambridge, 1931.

PASCAL, B. *Pensées*.

RINTELEN, J. V. *Beyond Existentialism*. London, 1961.

ROUBICZEK, P. *The Misinterpretation of Man*. New York, 1947.
  Thinking in Opposites. London, 1952.
  Thinking towards Religion. London, 1957.

INDEX

absolute, discussion of term, 1, 73–4, 153–4
absurd, the, 9, 106, 111, 166, 184
Angst, *see* dread
Augustine, St, 61
'authentic life', *see* life, 'authentic'

Bacon, Francis, 163, 165
Bataille, G., 118–19
Beauvoir, S. de, 125
Berdyaev, N., 91, 117
Bergson, H., 20
birth, problem of, 57, 118–20, 161
body and mind, 132–3
Bredsdorff, E. L., 108n
Buber, M., 116, 117, 139–60, 162, 184;
concept of grace, 144–5;
idea of God, 152–7, 160;
'individuality' and 'person', 149, 158;
and mysticism, 154–6, 160;
'personal meeting', 141–5, 148, 152;
'suffering and action', 145–6
view of society, 147–8, 151–2;
Buddhism, 76, 84, 153, 156n

Camus, A., 6, 15, 30, 117
Christianity, 9–10, 15, 18, 27–8, 34, 41,
47, 52, 56, 62, 66, 70–2, 90–1, 103,
106, 107–8, 144, 152, 157–8, 178–9;
see also morality, Christian
Commandments, Ten, 80, 83–4, 106,
156
Confucianism, 76, 84
Copernicus, 48

Darwin, 2, 19–24, 28, 35, 41, 79
death, problem of, 113–14, 135, 137,
161, 171
decadence, fear of, 30–1
Descartes, 8
despair, 54, 58–9, 61–2, 112–13, 114,
115, 123, 126–9, 137–8
determinism, 4–5, 14, 32, 47–8, 121–2
Dostoevsky, 31–2, 52–3, 69–70
dread (Angst), the concept of, 56–61,
112, 135, 137
Durkheim, E., 81

Eliot, T. S., 96
essence and existence, 11, 109–10, 119–21,
123–5
evolution, theory of, 2–3, 20–3, 26, 33,
35–6, 164
existence, *see* essence and existence
Existentialism, definition of, 10–11;
absolute, definition of, 110, 118

faith, *see* knowledge and faith
Farmer, H. H., 59n., 93, 117, 182
freedom of the will, 5, 13–14, 78, 121–3,
129;
see also necessity and freedom

Galileo, 163, 165
Gast, P., 51
genius, 68n., 149
George, Stefan, 31
Gestalt-psychology, 143–4, 149
God, 9, 13, 26, 104, 110, 152–7, 163,
178–9;
see also Nietzsche, 'God is dead'
grace, 144–5, 178–9
Guardini, R., 117, 132

Hamann, 8
Hartmann, Nicolai, 165
Hegel, 19, 20, 47, 55, 102, 131n.
Heidegger, M., 113, 115, 117, 123–4,
125–6, 129–37, 159, 160
Heisenberg, W., 2, 5n.
heroism, 34
history, 15, 49;
see also situation, historical
Hölderlin, 130, 132
Hoyle, F., 164
Hume, David, 84–5
Huxley, Julian, 3n., 21, 22, 32, 36–7

irrational, the, 49, 111–12, 115–16, 118,
161–84;
definition of, 161–2
I-Thou, 119–20, 140–60, 174, 177–8, 183

Index

Index